What readers are saying about Robert Lesslie's previous books

Angels and Heroes

"I am not one who likes to read, but when I started I could not put this book down...It made me realize that there are still good people on earth. I am a full-time police officer and a volunteer firefighter/EMS. I can't wait to pass this book on to others in my field."

Gary

"What stories are held in this book—people who just go the whole way to be a help and sacrifice their lives! I am not much of a reader of nonfiction like this...but I fell in love with this book."

—*GiveawayGal.blogspot.com*

Angels on Call

"These stories...are written with passion and love. Dr. Lesslie writes with clarity and enthusiasm. His stories will make you cry and laugh and will keep you on the edge of your seat."

—*ReaderViews.com*

"As an assistant principal...I have reflected on my own life's work with adolescent students as I read each account...I am writing to share how very much I enjoyed your book, especially the inspiring scriptural references accompanying each story."

Don

"Thank you for the...*amazingly awesome* books you have written. As a Christian pursuing a career in medicine, I find them really inspiring. I had tears in my eyes many times, especially in *Angels on Call*. I love, love, love these books!"

Alina

"The book was an inspiration during a difficult time in our lives...Your humility and humanity jumped out at me. I truly believe God works through us and that there are angels among us."

Chuck

Angels in the ER

"The most inspiring and relatable book I have read throughout my college career in nursing school...I often feel that my small contributions of extra time with patients or a simple smile have no impact on anyone's life. I was inspired by your book and appreciated the Bible verses throughout."

Katie

"I am a busy working mother but managed to read the entire book in less than three days. The way you described the people and the situations was brilliant...You see things in a very special way and have made me see... thank you."

Jamie

"Just read your book *Angels in the ER* and loved it. Couldn't put it down. Very well written. Excited to see another one is on the way! God bless you."

Bill

"Having spent ten years as a coordinator for our emergency department, I was very intrigued to read your stories...You have a very eloquent way of relating things that most people will never experience, but probably should...Your kindness, care, and compassion shine through."

Alicia

ANGELS
on the
NIGHTSHIFT

Robert D. Lesslie, M.D.

HARVEST HOUSE PUBLISHERS
EUGENE, OREGON

ANGELS ON THE NIGHT SHIFT

Copyright © 2012 by Robert D. Lesslie, MD
Published by Harvest House Publishers
Eugene, Oregon 97402
www.harvesthousepublishers.com

Library of Congress Cataloging-in-Publication Data
Lesslie, Robert D.
  Angels on the night shift / Robert D. Lesslie.
    p. cm.
  ISBN 978-0-7369-4842-5 (pbk.)
  ISBN 978-0-7369-4843-2 (eBook)
  1. Hospitals—Emergency services—Popular works. 2. Emergency medical personnel—Popular works.
  I. Title.
  RA975.5.E5L478 2012
  362.18—dc23

                                                                  2011051985

Printed in the United States of America

             12 13 14 15 16 17 18 19 20 / LB-CD / 10 9 8 7 6 5 4 3 2

To the memory of my mother,
Harriet Denton Lesslie. She believed in her son.
Proverbs 31:28-31

Contents

*Each of us will one day fall short and fail—
with our friends, our family, our work, or with ourselves.
Some of us will find forgiveness. Fewer still will find
redemption. It is a precious and costly gift.*

If Jesus Christ was who He claimed to be,
and He died on a cross
at a point in time in history,
then,
for all history past and all history future
it is relevant
because that is the very focal point
for forgiveness and redemption.

JOSH MCDOWELL (1939–)

1

It Begins

Tuesday, 7:14 a.m. "Dr. Lesslie, I need you in cardiac!"

Amy Connors and I looked over to the triage doorway and the fast-approaching wheelchair. Lori Davidson was behind it, a look of concern on her face as she turned down the hallway toward the cardiac room. The middle-aged man in the chair looked into my eyes, his face pale and fearful. He was leaning forward and tightly gripping the armrests.

"Chest pain," Lori called back over her shoulder.

I had been sitting behind the counter of the nurses' station, talking with Amy, our unit secretary. Her son Jackson was fast becoming a football star at one of our area high schools.

"I'll call for the lab," she said, reaching for her phone. "And I'll send Jeff in with the EKG machine. Anything else?"

I was already around the corner of the counter, following Lori and her patient.

"That should be okay for now," I answered her. "Let's see what's going on."

Lori was helping her patient onto the stretcher as I walked in. He glanced over at me and nodded his head.

"This is Ernest Shays, Dr. Lesslie," she told me, reaching behind her for the heart-monitor electrodes on the crash cart. "He started having some chest pain about an hour ago and drove himself to the ER. History of hypertension but no diabetes or heart disease."

She pressed the adhesive electrodes onto his chest, checked the monitor for good contact, then reached for some nasal prongs and plastic tubing.

"O2?" she asked, looking up at me.

Ernest seemed a little short of breath, and I nodded to her. "Three liters a minute." His color wasn't good, and he kept a hand pressed against his sternal area. "And let's get a line started."

I was about to ask for his blood pressure, when Lori said, "88 over 60 in triage. I'll check it again now."

The door opened and Jeff Ryan walked in. He was the nurse assigned to cardiac this morning, and he went quickly over to where Lori stood.

"What do you need?" he asked.

She handed him the oxygen setup and said, "If you'll get this going, I'll work on his IV. And we need to repeat his blood pressure."

I stepped to the other side of the stretcher and began asking Mr. Shays about his chest pain. Glancing over at the counter behind him, I noticed his short-sleeved shirt, tossed there by Lori. An open pack of Marlboros had partly slipped out of the breast pocket.

"I was fine when I got up this morning, Doctor," he was telling me. "Getting ready to go to work, when all of a sudden my chest started hurting. Never had anything like it in my life. It was terrible. Sharp pain, like I was tearing apart. Right here," he said, pointing to his breastbone. "After a couple of minutes, it seemed to ease off. But I felt weak, and knew I needed to get to the hospital."

Lori was behind me, getting a bag of normal saline from one of the shelves on the wall. I heard the sound of glass hitting the counter and jerked my head around. Two glass vials had fallen, apparently as she'd been sliding the bag toward her. She picked up one, which was cracked open and empty. The other one was empty as well. She held up the first one to the light and studied the label.

I noticed a puzzled look on her face and asked, "What is it?"

"It's Vistaril," she answered. "But I don't know what it's doing up here. Why would—"

"70 over 50," Jeff called out with an edge in his voice.

I turned back to the stretcher and said to Lori, "Let's get that line going."

She tossed the vials into a nearby trash can, grabbed her IV supplies, and quickly turned to Mr. Shays.

"I'm right here."

One of our techs hurried into the room, pushing our EKG machine. "Can I get in there and get this done?" she asked, looking over at Jeff. "Yeah," he answered, checking the patient's BP again.

He inflated the cuff and slowly released it, listening carefully. "Still 70 over 50."

"Are you having any pain now?" I asked Ernest.

"No pain, Doctor. I just feel weak, and a little light-headed."

"Do you want this wide open?" Lori asked me, having started the IV and now adjusting the flow rate.

"And my legs are gettin' numb," Shays added, looking up at me.

I looked over at the monitor. His heart rate was in the 80s and regular. Then I glanced down at the EKG that was printing and just starting to be spit out from the machine. It looked normal, with no evidence of any acute injury.

"I can barely feel them," Ernest said again, rubbing the tops of his thighs.

He was remaining calm, which was more than I could say about myself. He was in trouble and I was beginning to fear the worst.

"We need a portable chest X-ray stat," I directed Jeff, looking over at him and seeing his worried brow furrowed. He was feeling for a femoral pulse and nodded his head. "Faint, but I can feel it," he told me. "And I'll get Amy on that X-ray," he added, stepping toward the doorway.

"Wide open on those fluids," I told Lori. "And we need to get lab in here now. The routine stuff, but we're going to need to type and cross for some blood too."

She glanced at me, a question in her eyes.

"Is it my heart, Dr. Lesslie?" Ernest asked me. "Am I going to die?"

I stopped what I was doing and looked down into Mr. Shays's eyes. He was afraid, and I needed to be honest with him. If I was right, it wasn't his heart, but he was in real trouble.

"Ernest—" I began, but was interrupted by the appearance of the portable X-ray machine in the doorway. The radiology tech was deftly guiding the cumbersome motorized equipment to the edge of the stretcher.

"Ready for this?" she asked, already beginning to swing the arm and tube over Mr. Shays's chest.

"Yeah," I answered, stepping back out of her way. "We need that as fast as you can."

The chest X-ray would probably give me my diagnosis, and I still needed to answer Ernest's question. But that would have to wait.

"I'm going to step out into the hallway," I told him, patting his arm. "When she's finished, I'll be back in."

As I opened the door to leave, I was met by Amy Connors.

"Mr. Shays's wife and son just got here," she told me. "They're out in the waiting room and want to know if they can come back."

I closed the door behind me and we stepped into the triage hallway.

"Let them know we're getting a few things done, but they can come back in a couple of minutes," I said. "Give me a chance to look at that X-ray and then I can let them know more about what's going on."

A few minutes later, standing in front of the view box, I had my answer. Ernest Shays's chest X-ray was clearly abnormal, with a markedly widened mediastinum. This was the central part of his chest, which contained his heart, but also his major blood vessel—the aorta. It was enlarged, much bigger than it should be. The tearing feeling he had experienced was this big vessel ripping apart—dissecting. Like the rings of an onion, the inner lining was separating from the outside of the vessel, and the ripping was making its way through his chest and down into his abdomen, shearing off any blood vessels in its way. That's why his legs were getting numb. The arteries that supplied those limbs were no longer carrying blood to them.

His blood pressure had responded to the IV fluids we were giving him, providing a narrow but closing window to save his life. And his pain had gotten better after the initial dissection had started, after the ripping had begun its work. After that initial tearing sensation, most patients seemed to have a lessening of their pain. But that was a false sense of improvement. Things were going to get worse.

As I walked back to cardiac, I glanced over at Amy.

"Get me the thoracic surgeon on call," I said. "Tell him I need him right now. And you can let Mr. Shays's family come back. I want to talk with them."

Jeff was standing at the head of the stretcher, adjusting Ernest's IV tubing.

"Pressure's up to 90 over 60," he told me. And he says he's starting to feel his legs again. Do we need to do anything else?"

Prompted by the comment, Ernest moved his legs from side to side, patting his thighs. "I'm feeling better, Doctor," he said hopefully. His face was still pale, and the fear remained in his eyes. "What did you find out from the X-ray?"

The door opened and Amy ushered in a middle-aged woman and a young man who looked to be in his twenties, Mr. Shays's wife and son. They immediately stepped over to his side, his wife caressing his damp forehead and gently grasping his hand.

Then anxiously she looked up into my face.

"I'm Ernest's wife," she nervously told me. "And this is our son, Julius. Please tell us what's wrong with him. Is he going to be okay?"

I could see she was trying mightily to maintain her composure, but her lips were trembling as she said this. She could see how pale he was, and feel the clammy coolness of his brow beneath her hand.

Taking a deep breath, I began to explain what was causing Ernest's chest pain. His aorta was dissecting, and if he was going to live, it had to be repaired—and quickly. That "window" was now counted in moments, not hours.

"Is he going to—" Mrs. Shays began, interrupted by the door of cardiac bursting open.

Jason Evans, one of our thoracic surgeons, rushed into the room, dressed in surgical scrubs and still wearing a sweat-stained surgeon's cap. He must have just come out of the operating room.

"Robert," he stated with unusual animation. "I looked at the chest X-ray hanging on the view box. If that's his," nodding at Ernest Shays, "we need to get him to the OR right now."

"It's his," I confirmed. "And we've called the OR supervisor and let her know what's coming."

"Have you crossed him for some blood?" he asked, stepping over to the side of the stretcher and putting his hand on Ernest's shoulder.

"Eight units," Jeff told him.

"Good," Jason nodded. "But we're going to need more."

He quickly introduced himself to Ernest and then to his wife and son. As quickly as he could, he explained what needed to be done, and then he was gone.

The room erupted with activity. A nurse from the OR hurried in, while Lori helped Jeff make the necessary preparations to get our patient over to surgery. Another lab tech came in with several units of cross-matched blood. And all the while, Ernest lay on his stretcher, calmly holding his wife's hand and curiously surveying the hectic activity surrounding him.

Then he was wheeled out into the hallway toward the OR, and he was gone.

I stood in the middle of the now strangely silent and almost empty room, the floor littered with bits of cardiac monitor strips and discarded wrappers and pieces of equipment.

Mrs. Shays and her son stood next to me, staring at the floor and not knowing what to say or what to do.

Without raising her eyes, Mrs. Shays quietly whispered, "Dr. Lesslie, is Ernest going to live? Will we see him again?"

I looked at her and then over at her son.

"Dr. Evans is a good surgeon," I told her. "Your husband is in good hands."

Her head remained bowed for a few more seconds. Then she looked up and in a calm voice said, "He's in the Lord's hands."

I looked more closely at this woman. Her face now radiated peace and a sure knowledge of what she had just said.

"Yes, he's in the Lord's hands," I repeated.

2

Grace Under Fire

6:55 p.m. Elizabeth Kennick walked through the ambulance entrance, an overnight bag slung over her shoulder. She was the 7p to 7a doctor—my relief. As usual, her long blonde hair, light-blue eyes, and warm, self-assured smile caused most of the male heads in the department to turn in her direction.

She was used to the attention, and without seeming to notice it, she walked over to where I stood and plopped her bag on the floor beside me.

"Anything exciting to tell me about, Robert?" she asked, glancing over to the patient ID board. It was almost completely filled in, with only a few empty beds in the department. Typical for this time of day.

I was finishing up some prescriptions for the asthmatic truck driver in room 4.

"Nope," I answered. Then sliding the chart down the counter to Jeff Ryan, "This should just about do it for me, so there's nothing to turn over."

"Good," she replied, her voice animated with anticipation. "Looks like we're going to have a busy evening."

I had first met Elizabeth—Liz, as she preferred—when she was a fourth-year medical student rotating through the emergency department of Charlotte Memorial Hospital. I was serving as chief resident, and found her to be quick, eager, and a good Password partner at three in the morning. Nobody could beat us. Her parents were both physicians, internal-medicine specialists in Asheville, and she had finished summa cum laude at Chapel Hill.

After med school, she had completed an emergency-medicine residency in Atlanta, and then we had talked her into joining us in Rock Hill. After only three months, she had fit right in and was one of the "family."

"I guess no Password tonight," I quipped, then turned and headed down the hallway to our office. Liz grabbed her bag and followed me.

We were just outside the ortho room, about to turn the corner, when Jason Evans almost ran into me.

"Whoa, Robert!" he exclaimed, stopping just in front of me. "Glad I caught you. I wanted to give you an update on the guy with the thoracic dissection."

"Mr. Shays," I said. "Yeah, how is he doing? We haven't heard anything."

He stood silent for a moment, shaking his head. It was then I noticed the blood spattered on his pant legs and surgical shoe covers. His scrub top was drenched with sweat, plastered against his body.

"We just finished in the OR," he said, glancing over at Liz and then back to me. "That was a really close one. It took us forever to get enough exposure to find out where he was bleeding, and then to put things back together. But he's heading up to the ICU shortly, and he's stable, for the moment. He's not out of the woods, but he's got a reasonably good chance of surviving this."

Relieved, I nodded my head, then asked, "Is his family still in the surgical waiting room?"

"Just left them," Evans replied. He glanced down at his wristwatch. "Gotta get going. Got several people to see upstairs. Just wanted to let you know about your patient." Then he turned and was gone.

"You had a dissection today?" Liz asked, wide-eyed and excited. "And did he say *thoracic*? I've never seen one. How did he present? Was it straightforward or...You know, according to the textbooks, only 25 percent of them present with classic symptoms, and only 50 percent survive an operation. In fact, most don't make it to the OR."

She paused just long enough for me to wonder which question I was supposed to answer.

"Wow! You were right, Robert," she exclaimed. "You told me I'd see it all if I came to Rock Hill!"

She paused again, and I had just enough time to say, "I need to go check on Mrs. Shays before I head home. And you'd better get out to the department and keep things moving."

Heading toward the surgical waiting room, I heard our office door open behind me and Liz call out, "I want to hear all about that case in the morning!"

I shook my head, marveling at her enthusiasm and trying to remember if I had been that way when I first started out. Taking a deep breath, I walked down the hall toward the surgery waiting room.

Mrs. Shays and her son were sitting on the lone sofa in the small but brightly decorated room. They glanced up as I entered, and the initial smile of recognition on Mrs. Shays's face quickly faded into a look of concern.

"Is something wrong?" she asked hesitantly. "Dr. Evans said…Is Ernest…"

"No, no, Mrs. Shays," I reassured her, quickly stepping over to the nearest chair and sitting down. "Ernest is fine. I just talked with Dr. Evans, and your husband is in recovery and doing okay. He's gone through a lot today, and he's still critical, but he's alive. And we both know he's in good hands."

She smiled and gently patted her son's knee. Julius was staring silently at the floor, his shoulders hunched over.

"You people in the ER were so good to him, and…and Dr. Evans is…"

She stopped, choking back a sob, and looked away.

"It's okay, Mrs. Shays," I said, reaching out and putting my hand on her surprisingly frail and delicate shoulder. "I'm just glad we got to him when we did."

There was nothing else for me to say, and the three of us sat in silence for a few moments. Then I stood and walked to the door.

"I'll be back in the ER tomorrow morning," I told them. "When I get the chance, I'll go up to the ICU and check on Ernest."

As I opened the door to leave, she nodded her head, looked up at me once more, and quietly said, "Thank you."

I walked down one of the back hallways and out through a staff entrance. A short sidewalk led to the parking area, and I was almost at my car when someone called my name.

"Dr. Lesslie."

The voice was weak, almost muffled, and yet familiar. Whoever had called out to me was thirty, maybe forty feet away, and I turned in that direction.

"Dr. Lesslie," the call came again.

This time, I recognized the voice and the middle-aged man sitting in his wheelchair. He was being pushed toward the ambulance entrance by a woman, who I also recognized. It was Blaine Anderson and his wife, Mary Ellen.

"Blaine," I called out, walking over to the couple. "What brings you to the hospital this evening? I thought we had you pretty well tuned up when you were in the ER a couple of weeks ago. What happened?"

I reached down to shake his hand and almost recoiled in surprise. It was scorching hot, and terribly wasted. There was no strength in his grip at all.

Leaning over and studying his face in the pale light of the parking-lot lamps, I could now see that he was drenched in sweat. And then he coughed. It was more of a rattle, a gasp really, than a cough. I held onto his hand, troubled by his rapid decline in such a short time.

"Got some fever this evening, and this dang cough," he said with great effort, barely mustering something more than a whisper. "I think it's pneumonia again."

He was probably right, and I looked up at Mary Ellen. She stood behind her husband, and he didn't see as she slowly shook her head. She knew.

"Well, the two of you need to get into the ER." I glanced at the ambulance entrance and pointed in that direction. "Mary Ellen, why don't you take him through those doors? Just stand on the mat and press the button on the right side. Then just go on in and one of the nurses will show you where to take him."

I hoped there was still a bed open. Blaine couldn't afford to spend any time in the waiting room or in triage.

"Thanks, Dr. Lesslie," he murmured. "Wish you were going to be here tonight."

There was a brief moment of guilt and anxiety as I realized that Liz Kennick would be taking care of Blaine. But she knew her stuff, and she would recognize a sick patient when she saw one.

"Wish I could too, Blaine, but if I don't get home pretty quickly, I'll be in big trouble."

"Just kiddin'," he said, smiling weakly. "We'll be just fine."

They turned and headed to the ER. I watched them for a moment, remembering the first time I had met this courageous and doomed man.

It had only been a little more than two years earlier. The chart sitting on the countertop had read, *48 yr old M—laceration of left thumb.*

It had been a cold November morning, a Saturday, and Blaine Anderson and his wife were the only ones back in the minor trauma room. He was sitting on the stretcher in the back right corner and looked up sheepishly as I walked over.

"Well, what's going on here, Mr. Anderson?" I asked, sitting down on the rolling stool by his stretcher.

It was the first time I had ever seen this man, but I immediately knew there was something special, something different about him. In his face was a kindness, a gentleness that put me completely at ease.

He held up his bandaged and bloody hand, silently shook his head, and looked woefully up at his wife.

Mary Ellen introduced herself and explained, "Blaine was a little careless this morning. We have some friends coming over to watch a football game this afternoon, and he was helping make the chili. He got in a hurry, and the onions got the better of him."

Blaine was dressed in khakis, now blood-spattered, and a much-worn orange-and-purple Clemson sweatshirt.

"Tiger fan, I see." I nodded at his jersey and carefully picked up his injured hand.

He glanced down at his chest and then back up to me.

"Yep. And how about you? Not a Gamecock fan, are you?" he answered. Then smiling mischievously, "Don't want you to take out your troubles on me."

I chuckled while removing the hastily applied kitchen towel. "Nope. Went to Erskine, so I can pull for anyone I want."

"Good for you," Mary Ellen quipped. "A fall Saturday afternoon at our house turns a bunch of grown-up men into fourth-graders." She rolled her eyes down at her husband, then leaned closer and asked, "What do you think? Is he going to need stitches?"

I studied the exposed hand, examining the two-inch laceration over the back of his left thumb. His tendons were fine, and he could feel everything I was doing.

"He's done a pretty good number on himself," I answered. "Looks like a few stitches, but he'll be fine. Tell me how it happened," I asked, looking up at him.

It was one of those things that just barely registers somewhere in the back of your mind. Something that doesn't quite make it to the front of your consciousness.

When Blaine Anderson had looked at me, his eyes had flickered. It was brief, just a few up-and-down movements of his pupils. But it had been there. And then it was gone.

"Well, Dr. Lesslie," he began. "Contrary to what Mary Ellen is saying, I was *not* in a hurry, but was carefully slicing some red onions. I'm an electrical engineer, and I value my fingers, though it might not look like it this morning. But I'm really not sure what happened. Nothing slipped, and I was watching carefully. I just seemed to lose control for an instant. I must have lost my grip on the handle or something."

"Dr. Lesslie, EMS 2 is bringing in a chest pain, blood pressure of 80 over 40."

It was Lori Davidson, standing in the doorway behind me.

"They should be here in ten to twelve minutes," she added, then disappeared up the hallway.

"Let's get this numbed up," I told them. "And one of the nurses will start irrigating it while I check on that ambulance patient. Shouldn't take but just a little while, and then we'll get you back to your chili."

"Thanks, Doc," he said. "Do what you need to do. We'll be right here."

Blaine's thumb laceration healed well, and I didn't see him again for another five or six weeks. He and Mary Ellen came into the ER again, this time late one Wednesday night. He had been bothered with a right-sided headache all day, something he usually didn't experience. And then the pain moved and seemed to be centered in the back of his right eye, especially when he looked around.

"I wasn't too worried about this, Dr. Lesslie, until my vision started to get blurry," he explained. "It seems to have really gotten worse over the past couple of hours."

All of his vital signs were fine, his neck was supple, and he had no fever. A quick assessment of his neurological status didn't show up anything unusual. But his vision was significantly reduced in that right eye. He was almost completely blind.

"Have you had any trouble with your eyes?" I asked. "You're forty-eight now, and that's about the time things start to change."

"I've never had any problems," he quickly answered. "Never needed reading glasses or anything. Right up until this morning. What do you think's going on?"

Mary Ellen stepped closer to her husband and gently put a hand on his shoulder.

I walked over to the curtained opening of room 4 and switched off the light.

"Let's take a good look at that eye," I told them, stepping back to his stretcher and taking the ophthalmoscope from its holder on the wall.

First, I checked his "good eye," the left one. Carefully focusing the light beam on the back of the eye, I examined his fundus. The lining of that part of the globe can give you a lot of information about blood vessels and the optic disc, where the optic nerve enters the eye from the brain. You can also see a retinal detachment, which was something I was concerned about. Yet that really didn't fit his symptoms.

"This eye looks fine," I told him, leaning back and shifting over to examine his right eye. "Let's take a look at this one."

It took a few seconds to adjust the light so I could see his retina. It looked fine, and his blood vessels were normal here as well. Then I found his optic disc, and there was the answer.

I felt myself stiffen a little, and then focused more intensely on the small opening in the scope. Then I glanced away, paused, and looked back once more. I needed to be sure.

There was no mistaking what I was seeing. The disc was grossly swollen and pale, clearly different from the other side.

It all began to make sense now. I remembered the flickering of his eyes when he had come in with the lacerated thumb. And the momentary clumsiness he couldn't quite explain. After asking him about any unusual episodes of numbness in various parts of his body, things that seemed to "come and go," and getting a positive response from him, I was afraid I had the diagnosis. Or at least something that would have to be ruled out.

"Blaine, we're going to need to have one of the neurologists take a look at you. This might be the first signs of multiple sclerosis, and we need to find out."

The couple were stunned, and just looked at each other for a moment.

"But Dr. Lesslie, this is just a headache and some blurred vision," he stammered. "Isn't there something I can take and just..." He fell silent and looked down at the floor. He knew this was nothing simple and straightforward.

"I'm not saying that's what you have," I said, trying to reassure him, yet fearing that my instinct was correct. "You'll need to see a specialist and have some testing done to find out for sure."

My hunch had been correct. Within the week, Blaine Anderson had been given the diagnosis of multiple sclerosis, and it seemed to be a very progressive and aggressive form of the disease. His neurologist sent him to Johns Hopkins and the Mellen Center at the Cleveland Clinic for any ideas and help they might have. Their answers were the same. This was one of the most rapidly advancing cases they had ever seen, and even though they tried some of the most cutting-edge therapies available, no one was able to halt the onslaught of this debilitating illness. Blaine and Mary Ellen were left with dealing with the finality of his disease, and with its inexorable outcome.

But they weren't alone. Their family members and friends stood with them, as well as members of their church. The two of them rarely came to the ER without a least a few of their supporters. And they came in more and more frequently.

Yet their spirits remained positive, almost cheerful, and Blaine's inner fire always inspired us. And as we watched while he physically disappeared before our eyes, his spirit seemed to soar, and to dominate and rise above the disease that was conquering his body. We all knew where this path was ending, but somehow there was no longer any sense of sadness when he came to the ER with shortness of breath, or weakness, or fever. Rather, his presence was uplifting, and somehow reassuring. And we were glad he was still with us, if only for a little longer.

As I watched the Andersons disappear into the ER, I wondered if this would be Blaine's last visit.

6:58 a.m. The next morning, I relieved a surprisingly fresh-looking Liz Kennick. She was standing at the nurses' station, writing on the chart of the woman in room 5.

She looked up as I came through the ambulance doors.

"Good morning, Robert!" she greeted me. "Just finishing up this patient and I'll turn things over to you."

"Great," I answered, walking over and setting my briefcase down on the floor.

"Tell me about Blaine Anderson," I asked her. "The fella that came in just as I was leaving last night. Looked like he might have pneumonia."

Her brow furrowed briefly as she searched her memory, sorting out the dozens of patients she had seen during her shift.

"Oh, you mean the guy with MS?" she answered. "Yes. Nice guy. He *did* have pneumonia, and crumped right after he got back from X-ray. I had to intubate him, and he's on a ventilator up in the ICU. Pretty sick man," she said matter-of-factly, with no emotion in her voice. This was the first time she had seen Blaine, and she didn't know him. I could forgive her for not cherishing this man the way the rest of us did. "I'm not sure he's going to make it."

It was what I had expected. But I felt a heaviness, a sadness now, hearing these words. I would try to get upstairs sometime today and check on him.

Sins of the **Fathers**

8:25 a.m. "Dr. Lesslie, come into my office. We need to talk a minute."

It was Virginia Granger, standing just outside her office, and her request took me by surprise. I was at the nurses' station, right in front of Amy Connors. Amy looked up and silently mouthed, "You're in trouble now." She snickered, then looked back down at the ER log.

I frantically tried to think of what I had done to be on Virginia's bad pad. That was somewhere that no one, at least no thinking person, wanted to be. Virginia had been the head nurse in the ER for a lot of years, and she commanded the respect of everyone in and out of the department. Her training was that of a military nurse, and that demeanor and bearing had not been softened by her years in the "civilian sector." If you crossed the line somehow, you were going to hear about it.

Unable to come up with anything I might have done *recently*, I took a deep breath and headed over to her office.

"Close the door, if you would," she instructed me from behind her desk. She was drumming her fingers on its clean and ordered surface, impatiently waiting for me to do as I was told and to have a seat in front of her.

Dutifully complying, I sat down and asked, "What is it, Virginia? Is there a problem in the department?"

"No, not a problem," she answered, looking me squarely in the eyes. "I just want to be sure that we don't have one develop."

I nodded my head, wondering where this was going. Maybe I *had* done something. Then I remembered last weekend. That must be it! I had somehow figured out how to put the hospital paging system on hold, then told one of our new secretaries there was a call for her on that line. When she picked up the phone and pushed the button, she would be speaking throughout the entire hospital. It had worked better than I had hoped, with the young woman insistently asking, "Hello! This is Miss Jones! Who is this? I know you're there! Who is this?"

Lori Davidson had come to her rescue and hung up the receiver, pointing an accusing finger at me. Miss Jones fortunately never figured out what had happened.

That must be it. Someone had talked.

"Virginia, I—"

"Tell me what you think about Darren Adler," she interrupted.

"Excuse me?" I stammered, having been prepared to fall on my sword and plead *mea culpa.*

"Tell me what you think about Darren," she repeated.

Incredibly, I was off the hook. I slumped a little in the chair and took a deep breath. Then I quickly collected myself and focused on her question.

Darren Adler was one of our new nurses. Actually, he wasn't exactly *new*, since we had known him as a paramedic for eight years before he decided to go to nursing school. His goal had been to get his degree, spend some time upstairs in the ICU and CCU, and then come to the ER. He had done just that and had begun working with us two months ago.

"I think Darren is fitting in with the staff," I told her. "And he's doing a good job. Why? Is there a problem?"

I glanced down at her desktop and for the first time noticed the personnel file. On its label I was able to make out Darren's name and date of hire.

"No, not a problem," she answered, pursing her lips and peering intently at me over her black horn-rimmed glasses. It was always difficult to meet and hold her gaze, and I found myself feeling the uncomfortable need to break off. But I didn't and instead focused my eyes on her seemingly permanent bright-red lipstick.

"Not yet, anyway," she continued.

"What do you mean?" I asked, becoming curious. Darren had always been a solid paramedic, and he was now proving himself to be a good ER nurse. What kind of trouble could he have gotten himself into?

"You know he came from the ICU," she said, nodding her head and not waiting for a response. "According to Brenda Slater, he did a good job for her. Dependable, focused on his patients, good charting."

She paused for a moment and I waited. Brenda Slater was the ICU charge nurse, and had been from the time I had first come to Rock Hill. We had had a few run-ins over the years, always about getting our admitted patients upstairs in a timely manner. But we had always been able to work things out. She was strong-willed, as was Darren, and I was beginning to understand Virginia's concerns. She and Brenda were close friends.

"There was never any specific problem that I know of," she went on. "But Brenda has some concerns about his attitude and his respect for authority. Maybe it was all those years with the EMS. He *does* seem at times to be doing his own thing. And that might get him crossways with me. We don't have the time for that down here."

She was studying me now, and I continued to look squarely into her eyes.

"I understand what you're saying, Virginia," I told her. "That's the last thing we need, for Darren to lock horns with you. But I'm sure that's not going to happen. This is where he wants to be, and he's worked hard to get here."

"I think so too," she mused. Then without thinking, she reached up and adjusted the small, starched white nursing cap that was bobby-pinned to her dyed-black hair.

She noticed my eyes following her movement, and the beginning of a twinkle—

"Don't you even…" she snapped, quickly putting her hands back on the desk. She was the only nurse in the Western Hemisphere who still wore one of these caps. And whenever I thought I could get away with it, I'd give her a hard time about it.

"Anyway," she sighed, composing herself. "Just help me with that. Give him a little guidance if he needs it. We don't want things to get out of joint. He has the potential to be a good one for us."

"I'll do what I can," I said, standing up and pushing the chair back. "Thanks for the heads-up."

"Just hold on there," she said, pointing to my chair. "I want you to tell me about the Haskell baby."

I sat back down, wondering once again how she seemed to know everything that happened in the department. I guess that was her job, but this had occurred more than two weeks ago, and at three in the morning. Darren Adler had been working with me that night. Maybe that's why she wanted to know.

3:15 a.m. Darren had been out in triage and had suddenly burst through the door, glanced over at the nurses' station, and said to me, "Got a sick one here. I need your help!"

Then he bolted toward major trauma. In his arms was the listless body of a two-year-old boy. Right behind him was a young woman dressed in jeans and a tie-dyed T-shirt. Her face was bloated from crying and she looked over at me with panic and fear in her eyes.

Amy Connors sat upright in her chair as I quickly headed for trauma.

"This is Tyler Haskell," Darren told me while carefully putting the boy down on the stretcher. "And that's his mother, Sherry," he added.

I nodded in her direction and went around to the other side of the bed.

"What's going on?" I asked Darren.

The child was breathing, but had a strange, dusky color. He was clearly cyanotic, suffering from a critical lack of oxygen, and his eyes had rolled up into his head. I easily found a femoral pulse and then automatically began to gently palpate his abdomen.

"His mother tells me he's been sick for a couple of days, but started to get a lot worse tonight," Darren explained while attaching cardiac electrodes to the boy's chest. "Blood sugar is normal, but his pulse ox out front was 84. You want some O2?" he asked, already reaching for the oxygen mask.

An oxygen saturation of 84 percent was low, dangerously so. His level should have been above 95. He would need some oxygen, and I would need to find out why he was cyanotic.

"Yeah, put the mask on him," I instructed Darren. "And we'll need lab down here and X-ray. And get respiratory therapy—we'll need a blood gas too."

"Got it," Darren answered, moving quickly and efficiently.

I listened to Tyler's heart and lungs, checking for any unusual chest sounds or a heart murmur. Normal.

"Let's see if he pinks up a little with the O2," I said to Darren. Then turning to his mother, "Does he have any medical problems? Has he ever been in the hospital for anything?"

"No...no," she stammered. "He's always been real healthy. Never had anything more than an ear infection. Not until a couple of days ago."

"Has he fallen or hurt himself somehow?" I asked her.

"No, nothing like that," she said, shaking her head emphatically.

"Does he take any medication?" I continued.

"No, nothin'. Just some Tylenol yesterday and today, 'cause of the fever," she answered, shaking her head. "Is he goin' to be alright?"

I continued to examine Tyler, carefully rolling him onto his side and looking for any bruises or anything unusual. Everything looked fine. No help there. Then as I moved him back over, he moaned a little and I glanced up at his face.

"How long has this been going on?" I asked her, pointing to the boy's mouth.

Leaning down over her child she said, "That started right after the fever. He just started gettin' these blisters and then wouldn't eat or drink. They must be hurtin' him a lot."

"Wow!" Darren softly exclaimed, looking into the back of Tyler's throat as I gently held his tongue out of the way with a wooden blade. "Look at that!"

In his haste to get him back to the ER, Darren hadn't looked closely at the boy's face.

His lips and the entire inside of his mouth were covered with angry, red ulcerations. Some were bleeding, and a few on his lips looked infected. It was almost certainly a viral infection, but maybe the worst I had ever seen.

"No wonder he wasn't eating," Darren said.

"We couldn't get him to take anything at all today," Sherry volunteered. "And we tried everything."

"We?" I asked, looking over at the young mother.

"Yeah, me and his father, Jupiter. Jupiter Wells," she informed us.

The name sounded familiar, and I was trying to place it when Darren spoke.

"Jupiter Wells?" he asked her, repeating the name.

"Yeah, Jupiter," she answered matter-of-factly. "Do you know him?"

"No. Well, not exactly, but…isn't he in—"

"He got out last week," she interrupted him, avoiding his eyes and looking back down at her son. "He's been real good to Tyler, tryin' to take care of him and all."

That's why the name had sounded familiar. We had seen Jupiter Wells on quite a few occasions in the ER. Bar fights, motorcycle accidents, you name it. And Darren, having been with the EMS, would have seen him more than we had.

Interesting.

I stepped back from the stretcher and quietly stroked my chin, trying to put all of these pieces together. Here was a previously healthy two-year-old boy, with what looked like a viral infection of his mouth and an ominous cyanosis. And he was becoming progressively less responsive. No medications, no history of trauma. And other than his mouth and the bluish discoloration of his entire body, he had a normal exam. There was an answer here, something that should be obvious. But it was eluding me. What was I not seeing?

Darren started an IV while two lab techs came in and drew blood for a battery of tests. Then he did something unusual.

"Excuse me," he said to one of the techs. "Can I hold one of those tubes?"

He took one of the blood-filled vials and walked over to the corner of the room, directly below one of the bright ceiling lights. Then he held the tube up and studied it, rolling it from side to side between his fingers.

"Is that all you'll need right now?" one of the techs asked me.

I had ordered every test I could think of and said, "That should do it for now. We'll call if something changes."

I was watching Darren, wondering what he was up to, when Sherry Haskell asked me, "What do you think is wrong with Tyler? Is he going to be okay?"

The boy's color had not improved with high-flow oxygen, and I had examined his heart carefully again, searching for some evidence of a faint murmur or some reason for oxygen not getting into his blood. His lungs were working, and his heart was—

"Doc, come over here a minute."

It was Darren, and he was still studying the tube of blood, holding it up in the light. I walked over behind him and looked up.

At first, I wasn't sure what he was talking about. And then I saw it. It was the *color* of the blood. Instead of being red, it was brownish. Almost like…chocolate! That was it—that was the answer!

The combination of chocolate-colored blood and persistent cyanosis was associated with a type of chemical exposure that altered the iron in the hemoglobin molecule. Technically, the ferrous iron was converted to the ferric form, which bound to oxygen but wouldn't release it to the body's tissues. All of the oxygen in the world wouldn't help. It was called *methemoglobinemia*, and if the level of the ferric form got too high, you would die of asphyxiation. *Tyler* would die of asphyxiation. We needed to convert the ferric form back to the ferrous, and fast.

I stepped over to the door, opened it, and called over to Amy Connors.

"Get the pharmacy on the phone and tell them we need some methylene blue—and we need it right now!"

Closing the door behind me, I turned to my nurse. "Darren, have you ever given methylene blue before?"

"Read about it, but never given it," he answered honestly. "Can't be too difficult, though. It's just a liquid, right?" He was already reaching for the drug manual that we kept on one of the shelves in trauma.

"Yeah," I answered, scratching my head once again. The liquid would be given by IV and would quickly alter Tyler's hemoglobin, allowing it to carry oxygen normally throughout his body. And it would save his life.

But why was he having this problem? How had this happened? The only cases like this I had ever seen were from some industrial exposure—some kind of dye or other chemical. And the cause was almost always obvious. But I had never heard of it in a small child and couldn't think of what kind of exposure would have caused this.

One of the pharmacy techs came into the room and handed Darren a clear plastic medication bag filled with a dark-blue liquid. It was actually kind of pretty, and I wondered how Tyler's mother would react when she watched it course through the IV tubing and into her son's body. It was perfectly safe, and she would be able to watch as her boy pinked up. *That* was going to make her happy, and was going to relieve me.

Darren was preparing the methylene blue when he looked over at Sherry. "You said a while ago that Jupiter was 'trying to take care of' Tyler. What did you mean by that?"

"He was really bothered by the way Tyler was actin', with his mouth and all," she began to explain. "Jupiter kept puttin' a cold rag on his lips, and tried to get him to take ice chips, but he wouldn't have none of it. Just kept turnin' his head away. That's when Jupiter went into the bathroom and came back with that spray."

Darren and I both jerked our heads in her direction.

"The spray?" I repeated, surprised by this answer. Maybe this—

"Good Lord!" Sherry exclaimed, pointing down to her son's arm. The methylene blue had filled the IV tubing and was starting to flow in. I understood her reaction. It was unusual and unexpected, and actually pretty bizarre. But it was necessary and would save her son. I explained all of this to her, and then Darren asked, "What 'spray' are you talking about?"

Sherry had relaxed a little, and looked up into Darren's face.

"It was some spray Jupiter had. He said it was for sore throats."

Darren and I looked at each other, and then he turned to Sherry again.

"What did it look like—the container, I mean?" he pursued.

She had a puzzled look on her face as she tried to remember.

"It was yellow, I think, with some thin metal tube comin' out the top. It was bent over, and when Jupiter pushed down on it, the spray would come out the end. Why? Was that somethin' bad? It seemed to help Tyler, at least for a while, so we kept usin' it."

Cetacaine—must be! I thought. That would explain it. Cetacaine was a topical spray we used to numb up someone's mouth or throat for an oral procedure we might be doing. And it could be used for pain relief. It contained a chemical, benzocaine, that was safe in small amounts. But used in excess, it could cause methemoglobinemia, probably especially so in small children.

"Where did he get the Cetacaine?" Darren asked her.

Sherry blushed and lowered her eyes. It wasn't critical to know this, but now I was curious. I didn't think you could get this stuff at the drugstore, and we always tried to keep a handle on it in the ER. I wondered how Jupiter happened to have it in his bathroom.

"Sherry?" Darren prodded gently.

She looked up at me and then at the nurse.

"He…he told me that it was good stuff, that they had used it on him one time in the ER when he had his mouth busted, and that he…he…"

She stopped, and we waited.

"He said that when the doctor and nurse left the room, he put it in his pocket."

There. She had said it, and now she visibly relaxed.

I shook my head, but wondered why I was surprised. This kind of thing happened all the time in the ER—surgical instruments, sterile gloves, medications, even a thermometer once.

"We've been missing a wheelchair…" the nurse whispered in my ear.

"Darren," I corrected him, chuckling.

Tyler had responded quickly to our treatment. He was much more alert and no longer had that dusky blue color when we sent him upstairs to the pediatric ICU. He would be discharged from the hospital in a few days, completely normal, active, and back to himself.

"What made you check out that blood?" I asked Darren while we stood together in the trauma room.

"I don't know, Doc. Something just seemed a little odd about all of this. And when I caught a glimpse of one of those vials, I knew something was up. Wasn't sure what, but it just wasn't right."

"Well, I'm sure glad you did," I told him as we walked back to the nurses' station. "I was really struggling with that one."

"Sounds like Darren Adler saved your bacon," Virginia said, once more peering over her glasses at me.

"I'll be the first to admit it," I said, standing up again, this time determined to make it back out to the department.

"I want to keep him down here," she said again. "I know you like him, but that will make it difficult for you to remain objective. Just keep your eyes open."

There was a faint knock on the door and I turned around.

Lori Davidson stuck her head in the room and said, "Have you got a minute, Ms. Granger? And you too, Dr. Lesslie?"

I looked back at Virginia and then down at my watch. I had been here for a while.

"The ER's quiet right now," Lori said, noticing me glancing past her shoulder. "This will just take a second."

"Sure, Lori," Virginia told her. Then motioning to one of the chairs, "Have a seat."

Lori walked over and took one of the chairs. Once again, I sat down and folded my hands.

"What is it?" Virginia asked.

"It may be nothing," she began quietly, clearly troubled. She was not an alarmist, and not one to cause a stir when there was no need for one. She had some good reason for concern.

She reached into the pocket of her jacket and took out three medicine vials. Their tops had been broken off and they were empty.

She leaned forward and put them down on the desk. Virginia reached over, picked up one of the vials, and studied its label.

"Vistaril," she said flatly, then waited for Lori to explain.

"Yes, it's Vistaril. And I found them behind a glove box on one of the shelves in the GYN room."

She didn't say anything more, but just looked at her head nurse.

"What in the world would they be doing back there?" Virginia asked. I was wondering the same thing, and then I remembered the medicine vials that had fallen on the counter the other day in cardiac.

"It might be a simple mistake," Lori replied. "Someone not thinking. But we don't use much Vistaril with our GYN patients, and with the vials I found in cardiac—"

"The what?" Virginia interrupted her.

Lori told us about the used vials of Vistaril she had found in the cardiac room.

"I don't remember anything like this ever happening in our ER," the young nurse said quietly.

This was troubling. Vistaril wasn't a significant "drug of abuse," yet we had seen far stranger things happen. And where there was smoke, there was usually fire. It was possible that someone in the department had a problem and was somehow abusing this drug. *Something* was going on, and whatever it was, we needed to figure it out.

I had been looking intently at Lori, and now my eyes moved over to the desk in front of me and down to the personnel file lying there. When I looked up, Virginia's eyes were fixed on mine.

4

The Other Side

Thursday, 3:30 a.m. Amy Connors sat in her chair at the nurses' station, organizing the patients' charts from the past evening. We had seen a bunch of people, and the stack in front of her was thick. But she had been doing this for a while, and seemingly without effort she filed each record in its proper place.

Jeff Ryan and I sat on each side of her, drinking coffee, catching our breaths, and silently watching her. We had emptied the department and were waiting for whatever might find its way through the doors.

Then Jeff said, "Doc, you know, I just love watchin' people work."

Without looking up, Amy replied, "Aren't you supposed to be doin' something? Or at least be somewhere else?"

"Nope," he answered, leaning back further in his chair and smiling over at me. "I'm supposed to be right here watchin' you."

The two had worked together for more than ten years and were good friends. They were both in their late thirties, and at first, I had thought it a bit of an odd relationship. Jeff Ryan was a big, strong, quiet man. He didn't have a lot to say, but when he did, it was usually something important. A lot of people were intimidated by his size and by the seriousness with which he approached his work. With Amy it was different, and with her he seemed to let his hair down. He talked with her more than with anyone else in the department.

That part was understandable. Amy Connors was wide open, gregarious, completely unassuming. You knew where you stood with her, and if she thought you didn't—well, she would quickly explain it. Maybe what they say about opposites is true after all. Whatever the reason for their friendship, it was always comfortable working with the two of them.

Amy shifted her chair, facing more toward me now, with her back toward Jeff. Without a word, she just kept filing.

"I'm just watchin' too, Amy," I told her, nodding my head.

She jerked up and looked straight at me.

"What the…Why do I have to put up with *both* of you tonight? What have I done?"

I laughed, then looking down I noticed a colorful, shiny brochure beside her stack of papers. On the cover was a GM Silverado truck, the big one, with an extended cab.

"What's this?" I asked her, pointing to the brochure.

"None of your business," she snapped impishly, turning over the brochure. "We just bought a new truck and I was goin' to take you guys outside and let you see it, but you can forget that!"

Clara Adams walked up just in time to hear this last exchange. She was a recent graduate from the nursing program in Columbia and had been working in the ER for a few weeks. I was afraid she might be too young and naïve to handle these two.

"What's going on?" she asked.

"We're just making sure Amy gets her work done," I told her. "And she seems to be taking it personally. Have a seat while you can," I added, motioning to one of the empty chairs on the other side of Jeff. "And tell us how you like working the night shift."

Clara walked around the counter and sat down. Jeff scooted his chair back, giving her more room. She was still in her mid-twenties—pretty, bright, and really animated. Her enthusiasm was contagious, except maybe for Jeff. He leaned back in his chair again, folded his arms across his chest, and slowly began rocking back and forth.

"It's been great!" she answered, smiling and leaning forward in her chair. "The night-shift staff people have been really helpful, and I've been able to sleep during the day. I wondered a little about that, but it's been fine. And the patients that come in during the middle of the night have been…" She stopped mid-sentence, a perplexed look on her face. She seemed to be struggling for just the right word. "Well, they've been very interesting."

Jeff continued to rock in his chair and didn't say anything. Amy had finished her filing and leaned back in her chair, folding her hands behind her head.

"Whatcha mean by that?" she asked the young nurse.

Clara took a deep breath and looked over at the secretary. Then she quickly glanced at Jeff and then at me.

"Well, it just seems that the people who come in during the middle of the night are really sick, or they are…they are…"

"Peculiar." Jeff finished the sentence for her.

"Yes. I suppose that's as good a word as any," she said, smiling and nodding her head. "They do seem to be a little…peculiar. I mean, they have some really odd problems, and some different personalities. You almost want to take some of them home with you."

"Now *you're* the one who's peculiar," Jeff said, his face expressionless.

"Well, if anybody should know peculiar, that would be *you*," Amy said, looking over at him.

As if she hadn't heard this, Clara took a deep breath and said, "Just the other night, I was taking care of a man in cardiac. He was having a heart attack and Dr. Kennick was taking care of him. One time when she went out of the room, the man looked up at me and asked if I believed in heaven. Now that made me stop what I was doing and pay attention."

Jeff stopped rocking and cocked his head in Clara's direction.

"Of course I told him I did," she went on. "And I said, 'What about you?'" She paused and looked over at me. "I hope it was alright to do that."

I nodded my head without saying anything.

"Well, he told me that he did too, and then he started telling me about his wife, and how just before she died, she told him that she could see a light. And she said that the light was something good, and not frightening. And she asked him if he could see it. Then he asked me what I thought about all of that."

"What did you tell him?" Amy asked her, listening intently.

"Before I could say anything, Dr. Kennick came back in the room, and we never had a chance to talk about it anymore. I wanted to find out more of what his wife had been talking about, but we didn't have the chance."

Clara grew quiet and we all just sat there.

"Peculiar," Jeff said, finally breaking the silence.

"No it's not peculiar," Amy scolded him. "If you believe in heaven, then you'd think there might be some sign...some sort of evidence or experience or something like that. You hear all the time about people who have passed over and come back. There was a special on TV not too long ago about that. But I don't know what to make of it, not havin' experienced it myself. What do you think, Dr. Lesslie?"

I was deep in thought, listening to the conversation and wondering about this phenomenon myself. All of my years in the ER had convinced me that life is a mystery and is truly fleeting. And I believe that our existence after we "cross the bar" will be beyond anything we can imagine. After all, as my wife frequently reminds me, once we are absent from this body we will be present with the Lord. Yet that moment of passage from this world to the next is another mystery. We have some rough blueprints maybe, but there are no videos or recordings, no soundtracks or DVDs. And that's probably the way it should be—a mystery.

"Dr. Lesslie," Amy persisted, interrupting my thoughts. "What do you think about this?"

They were all looking at me, and I sat up a little straighter and cleared my throat.

"Well, these near-death experiences are fascinating," I began. "And I'm not sure that until the 'final trumpet' blows, any of us will have the right answer. But there are some interesting stories out there, and some that are hard to argue with."

"Can't prove 'em though, can you?" Jeff interjected. "I mean, there's just no solid evidence about any of this, the lights and all."

I looked at him and said, "I really don't know what to make of most of it. But I can tell you about one instance I know of, and that *still* seems real to me, even after more than fifteen years. Maybe *more* so because of those years."

"What do you mean 'more so'?" Amy asked.

"Well, like I said, this happened fifteen, twenty years ago," I began. "Right here in this ER. Johnny Gee was working in the ER that day, and he told me—"

"See!" Jeff interrupted. "You got this secondhand. I thought this was going to be something *you* experienced," he said doubtfully.

"Just listen, Jeff," I replied patiently. "You'll see."

2:30 p.m. It was a spring afternoon, one day in the middle of the week. Johnny Gee was the ER doctor on duty and was standing at the nurses' station, reviewing the run report of EMS 2. The paramedics on the unit that day were Rob Freeman and Greg Hartley. They had just brought in a teenage boy who had tried to drive his four-wheeler through a pine tree. No major injuries, though, and he should be fine. Just a routine call and transport.

The whole day had been routine—nothing out of the ordinary. And that had been fine with Rob and Greg. They had been working together for a lot of years, and were both now in their early fifties.

Hartley was the more serious of the two. He was a deeply spiritual man, always calm and patient in the face of even the worst catastrophe, and never afraid to share his faith. Yet, as St. Francis of Assisi would say, he preached the gospel "without words."

Rob Freeman, on the other hand, was a free spirit, though less so now that he was getting a little older and had two grandchildren. But still, he didn't take many things very seriously. Certainly his job, but in spite of all their years together as EMS partners, Greg had never been able to draw Rob into a serious conversation about his beliefs. He just wasn't interested. That didn't make him a bad person to be around. In fact, he was one of the people best liked by the ER staff—always laughing and joking, and always ready to lend a hand wherever it was needed.

They made an interesting pair, and were two of our favorites.

On this particular day though, they had something important on their minds. It was already past two o'clock and they hadn't had a chance to get anything for lunch. There had been a series of minor calls all morning long, and now for the first time, they didn't have anything pending.

"See you guys in a little while," Gee said as the two were walking out of the building.

"Hope it's not before we get something to eat," Rob called back to him, stopping in the ambulance entrance and rubbing his less than svelte belly.

"Come on, Rob," Greg said to his partner. "I'm hungry."

The two men walked out under the portico of the ambulance entrance and toward their unit. Greg went around to the driver's side and jumped in, while Rob walked to the passenger side. As if choreographed after all their years together, they settled into their cushioned but well-worn chairs, buckled their seat belts, and adjusted their side mirrors. Greg cranked up the reluctant diesel engine, and they lumbered out through the parking lot and onto Herlong Avenue.

"Where you want to get lunch?" Greg asked his partner. He was checking his side mirror, making sure no one was behind him as he got ready to move into a turn lane and onto Ebenezer Road.

Looking ahead again, he repeated, "Rob, what do you want for lunch?"

It was a simple question, one about food, which was something Rob Freeman was always interested in.

There was still no response, and when Greg glanced over to the right, he slammed on the brakes of the ambulance, causing it to swerve in the middle of the street.

Rob Freeman was sitting up in his seat, held in place by his seat belt. But his head was hanging down on his chest, rolling from side to side. His face was a dark blue, and he wasn't breathing.

Hartley yelled at him, reached over and shook him, and instantly knew he had a decision to make. Did he stop in the street, pull his partner out of the cab, and start doing CPR? Or did he head back to the ER, a little over a minute away?

He didn't hesitate. Switching on his lights and siren, he made a U-turn in the middle of Ebenezer, scattering startled drivers out of the narrow road, and sped back to the hospital. Repeatedly blasting his horn as he approached the ambulance entrance, he got the attention of some of the staff.

Within another minute or so, Rob Freeman was on a stretcher in the cardiac room with Dr. Johnny Gee standing over him.

"Flatline," Angie Weathers told Gee. She was one of the nurses on duty this morning, and was trying to maintain her composure. Like everyone else in the department, the man dying in front of her was a friend, someone special.

Gee went to work, barking orders, securing Freeman's airway, and doing everything he was trained to do to save this man. *What could have caused him to collapse so suddenly? He doesn't have any history of heart disease and he doesn't smoke. He doesn't take any medications. It must be his heart. But what about a pulmonary embolus?*

Greg Hartley stood in the doorway of cardiac, trying to stay out of the way. He felt helpless, not wanting to watch this but unable to make himself leave.

For over an hour they worked feverishly. Every once in a while, an irregular complex or two would appear on the monitor and then quickly disappear. And then once again there was that awful flatline.

Everyone in the room knew it was time to stop. Johnny Gee, flushed and sweating, knew it too. He was about to call the code and pronounce the death of Rob Freeman, when suddenly the cardiac monitor erupted with activity. Freeman's failing heart was making one last attempt to keep him alive. The irregular complexes were coming more frequently, and then they became less irregular. In another minute or two he had a normal rhythm of about a hundred, and he had a pulse!

Gee stood back from the stretcher as Rob began to breathe on his own through the endotracheal tube taped to the side of his face. The doctor looked over at Angie Weathers and they just stared at each other.

Then Rob's right hand went up in the air as he reached for his face and the aggravating tube. Angie quickly grabbed his hand and happily secured it to the side of the stretcher.

An hour later, Rob Freeman was sitting up in his bed and talking. Amazingly, he seemed to be completely normal. Over the next few days, his cardiologists would determine that he had a rare and usually fatal electrical problem in his heart. He had successful surgery and never had any more trouble with it.

"Wow, that's a great story!" Amy interrupted me. "Maybe even a miracle. I've never met Rob Freeman but I've heard some of the guys talk about him. But it really doesn't have anything to do with what we're talkin' about, does it?"

"Well, just hold on, Amy," I said patiently. "I'm not finished yet. The *real* miracle might be what happened next."

After all the excitement, Johnny Gee found himself alone in the cardiac room with Freeman. He was writing on Rob's chart, hesitant to leave the room for fear that something might happen to undo what had just transpired.

"Doc, I gotta tell you something," Rob said quietly.

Johnny looked over at the paramedic. "Sure, Rob. I'm right here."

Freeman cleared his throat, trying to collect his thoughts. He was obviously struggling with something—some difficult emotion.

"I need to tell you what just happened," he said finally.

This surprised Johnny. He hadn't left the room since Rob's arrival in the ER, and he knew everything that had happened. He pulled over a stool, sat down, and waited patiently for his patient to continue.

Freeman took a deep breath and began.

"I've heard people talk about 'near death' experiences, but never paid them much attention. I always thought those people were crazy. But Doc…well, I *know* it's true now. I just don't know any other way to explain this."

He paused and glanced over at Johnny Gee, hoping for some sign of understanding. Or at least some sign that Johnny didn't think he was crazy.

Gee just looked at him, smiled, and nodded his head. That was all Rob needed.

"It's hard for me to put into words. But heck, here it is. From the first moment I got to the ER, when Greg brought me in on our stretcher, I can remember everything."

Johnny Gee's eyebrows rose, but he said nothing. He only shifted a little on his stool. This man had been unconscious—completely unresponsive.

"I can remember the whole thing," Rob continued. "I could hear you talking and giving orders, and I could hear Angie Weathers over in the corner. 'Flatline,' she kept saying. And I can remember somehow seeing the cardiac monitor, and it *was* flatline. But somehow that didn't bother me. It was all so peaceful, and I just watched and listened. It wasn't like I was floating on the ceiling like I've heard other people talk about. It was more of…more like just being in the room, but not *in* the room. Does that make any sense, Doc? I told you this was hard to understand."

Johnny nodded again and said, "Go on."

"Well, that's when it got stranger. I could hear you and Angie talking and then your voices started to sort of fade away. Not completely, but you were getting harder to hear and understand. And the room started to get sort of hazy, or cloudy. And it was getting darker. That's when I saw the light. It seemed to be over near the doorway, and I thought someone else might be coming into the room. But the door was closed, and I remember thinking, *It's just like they all say,* you know, the light and everything. And I laughed at myself a little for thinking that. Funny, but I remember laughing."

He paused, put his hand to his chin, smiled faintly, and shook his head.

"Then your voices got louder," he continued. "And the room got brighter and the light started to fade away. It was about that time that Angie hollered out that there was some electrical activity on the monitor, but she still couldn't feel a pulse. Things started getting darker again, and then there was the light. After a minute or two, it faded away again and I could hear you guys plain as day. This happened a couple more times until finally things got dark, really dark, and you guys were gone and I couldn't hear anything. It seemed like I was all alone.

"And the light…well, it really got bright. The brightest yet. I found myself being drawn toward it, walking straight at it. Not like a magnet or anything like that, or something I couldn't resist. It just felt comfortable, and…like something I was supposed to do. It was the only thing in the room, the only thing in the world right then—this bright light.

"Then all of a sudden, there he was, right smack in the middle of it. I could see the figure of a man, clear as you are right now. He just stood there, watching me. I remember being surprised, and I must have stopped, 'cause he raised his hand and motioned for me to come to him. I started walking forward again, thinking of all the times people had talked about something like this, and now I understood. I knew they weren't crazy, or making stuff up. It was just natural, and peaceful. And I began to remember the things people had said about heaven and about meeting Jesus and their loved ones, and it was…it was like I was just floating toward him—completely at peace."

Rob stopped here and looked down at his hands, and Johnny thought he saw tears in his eyes. Then the paramedic trembled a little. It was a slight movement, and passed quickly.

He wiped his eyes with the back of his hand and looked up again at the doctor.

"Then there I was," he continued, his voice now subdued. "I was standing right in front of him. I looked up and into his face, and it was…it was the face of a wolf. And Doc, I have never been so scared in all of my life. Those eyes, they were mean, and bright red, and it was like there was all of this hatred behind them. And then the feeling I got was that they were hungry."

He paused again, took a deep breath, and blew it out loudly.

"That's the first time in my life that I've ever felt fear, *real* fear. But it was more than that, Doc. It was an emptiness, a gnawing sort of pain, and the worst thing—the *worst* thing was that I knew I was lost. Then from somewhere behind me, I heard your voice again, and I heard Angie saying, 'Look, he's got a rhythm back, and I can feel a pulse.' The room started getting brighter, and the light started to fade, and then your voices started getting louder and louder. And that wolf, or whatever it was, just stood there, reaching out for me and grinning. But it wasn't really a grin. It was…I don't know. And then it was gone. And I was lying on the stretcher, looking straight up at the ceiling. And I was breathing."

Johnny Gee and Rob Freeman looked at each other in silence. Then Rob said, "Doc, I know that sounds crazy, but what do you think? Do you think what I saw was real?"

Johnny looked him square in the face, struggling with what he had just heard. "What do *you* think, Rob?"

Without hesitating, Rob answered, "I *know* it happened. Just as sure as I'm talking to you right this minute, I *know* it happened."

Johnny slowly began to nod his head. This *did* sound crazy—but Rob Freeman had just described in perfect detail the account of his own resuscitation. How do you explain that?

I stopped and just sat there. All of us were quiet, each wrestling with our own thoughts. It was Jeff Ryan who spoke first.

"That's quite a story. But how can you know it was real? I mean, there's no way of knowing for sure, is there?"

He was looking at me, and then they all were.

"What do you think, Doc?" Amy asked quietly.

"I'll tell you what I think," I began, scooting up to the edge of my chair and leaning forward, my forearms resting on my thighs. "And it's based on the only *facts* we really have, and that's what happened next."

"What do you mean?" Clara Adams questioned.

"Well, after Rob Freeman got out of the hospital, he went straight to the director of EMS and turned in his resignation. No questions, no explanations, nothing. Just thanked the director and walked away from all those years. Then he started talking to Greg Hartley about what he was thinking of doing, and asked him for some advice. Within a few weeks, he signed up for some college-level courses at York Tech, and a year later, he was in seminary. A few years after that, he became a minister."

"He did what?" Amy exclaimed, sitting straight up in her chair. "He became a preacher? I thought he didn't—"

"It all changed that day in the ER, Amy," I told them. "Whatever happened in the cardiac room, it was absolutely real for Rob Freeman, and it changed his life. He's been preaching ever since in a small church just outside of Lancaster."

"Wow," Clara whispered, staring at me.

Jeff Ryan didn't say anything, but he was nodding his head.

"I talked to Greg Hartley about this once," I added. "He said every word of it was true, and that Rob was a new man from that moment on. I remember him grinning at me when he said, 'Rob was bound and determined to never face that wolf again. And you know, Doc, he never will.'"

5

No Más

6:20 a.m. The remainder of the night had remained quiet, and I told Jeff and Amy I was going up to the ICU to check on a couple of patients.

"Page me overhead if you need me," I told them as I headed to the back of the department. "I won't be very long."

The staff elevator was empty as I went up to the third floor, to the ICU. I thought about Blaine Anderson and wondered what I would find there. And as the doors of the elevator opened, I remembered Ernest Shays and his torn aorta. I hadn't heard any more about him.

I stepped out of the elevator and turned right, heading to the back entrance of the unit. Charlotte Stanley looked up as I walked through the automatic doors and toward the nursing station.

"Dr. Lesslie, what brings you up here?" she asked, pushing back in her chair from the desk. "We don't have a code going on, do we?" she quipped.

Charlotte and I had worked together for a lot of years in the ER. She had wanted a change and was now the assistant director of the ICU. We missed her downstairs.

"Let me guess," she answered herself, reaching over to the patient chart rack. "You want to see Mr. Anderson, I bet."

She picked up the chart for room 6 and held it out to me. I could read "Anderson" on its dark-green front.

"Thanks," I told her, taking the chart and sitting down in one of the rolling chairs next to her. "How is he doing?"

"Not too good, I'm afraid," she answered quietly, glancing over in the direction of his cubicle. "He's been on the vent since he got here, and we've had to keep him pretty sedated. Can't keep his blood pressure up without a bunch of meds, and his kidneys have shut down. Dr. Dryer doesn't think it will be much longer."

I looked up from Blaine Anderson's chart, suddenly struck by the finality of this statement. Bill Dryer was a good pulmonary specialist and knew his stuff. I had known when I saw Blaine outside the ER that he was in bad shape—but still, it wasn't easy hearing this pronouncement.

"Hmm," I sighed, standing and putting the chart down on the counter. "I'll just take a look at him, if that's okay."

"Sure, no problem," she told me, sliding her chair up to the desk again and continuing her charting. "Take your time."

The overhead light was off in room 6 and it took me a moment to get used to the darkened cubicle. I tried to pull the curtain closed behind me as quietly as possible.

I was standing at the foot of the bed and was beginning to make out the slender, wasted form of Blaine Anderson, lying unmoving beneath his single sheet. Several kinds of muffled "beeps" were competing with each other from the head of his bed—the monitors of the ventilator and several other machines. Without thinking, I caught myself counting the number of his tubes. Somewhere along in my training, a senior resident had once informed me that if a patient had more than seven tubes exiting his body (IVs, Foley catheter, nasogastric tube, and so on), it was a sure sign they wouldn't survive. *Six.* I counted six tubes, so Blaine might still have a chance, though only a very small one.

That was absurd, and I was wondering why I remembered stuff like that, when a movement in the corner of the room drew my attention. It was Mary Ellen Anderson, stirring in her recliner on the other side of the bed. An open book was lying in her lap, and her head hung sleepily on her chest. She must have somehow sensed my presence and was slowly looking in my direction and struggling to get her eyes open.

"Dr. Lesslie," she whispered, glancing over at the clock on the far wall. "Good morning."

I walked around the foot of the bed and stood in front of her. In hushed voices we talked for a few minutes about her husband. She remained hopeful that he would once more "pull through this" and that they would be going home in a few days. That wasn't going to happen, but it wasn't for me to tell her.

"You need to be sure to take care of yourself," I said, stepping toward the curtain and taking it in my hand.

"I'll be fine," she answered. Then looking down at her husband, "We'll be fine."

I stepped out into the unit and pulled the curtain closed behind me. Charlotte was glancing over the counter at me and shaking her head. Then she looked back down at her work.

Halfway to the nurses' station I was startled to hear, "Dr. Lesslie! Hey, Dr. Lesslie!"

The voice was coming from behind me, from room 4, two cubicles down from Blaine Anderson.

I turned and walked in that direction.

Ernest Shays was sitting straight up in his bed, his oxygen tubing secured to his nose and his IV attached to his left hand, which was now beckoning me.

"Come over here a minute," he said in a forced whisper. He had seen Charlotte's stern look when he had first called my name.

"I was askin' about you the other day," he told me, pointing to the lone chair in the cubicle. "Have a seat if you've got a minute."

"I've got just a minute," I told him, stepping over to his bed and shaking his hand. "Got to get back down to the ER, but I'm glad I got to see you." I meant it—seeing him like this lightened my dark and heavy mood.

Ernest looked great. His color was good and his breathing was unlabored.

"Well, I'm glad you came by," he said cheerfully. "I wanted the chance to thank you for what you all did in the ER. Wouldn't be here today if it wasn't for you guys. And hey, I'm supposed to be moved to a step-down unit later on today! How about that!"

He was grinning as he said this, and I found myself smiling as well.

"That's great, Ernest," I told him. "You look like you're doing fine."

"It's a miracle, Doc, a flat-out miracle. Shouldn't be alive, but hey, here I am!"

I glanced over at the wall clock—6:50.

"Ernest, I've got to get back downstairs," I told him, moving away from the bed. "Don't take things too fast now," I warned him. "You don't want to go backward."

"Don't worry about that, Doc," he answered quietly, his eyes stealthily moving in the direction of Charlotte Stanley. "These nurses ride me like a bunch of bulldogs."

"That's what they're supposed to do," I chuckled, stepping out of the room.

"See ya later, Doc," he called after me.

I had counted only four tubes. He would be okay.

As I turned the corner and headed for the nurses' station, there stood Virginia Granger. It was an all-too-familiar pose, her feet apart, hands on hips, and her unwavering stare boring into me. If it was possible, it seemed that her starched white dress was brighter than usual.

"Good morning, Dr. Lesslie," she said pleasantly enough as I walked up beside her. I glanced up at the clock—five 'til seven—about the time she usually arrived in the department.

"Good morning, Virginia," I responded. "Is everything okay?" I always had the sense when I stood before her like this that she was going to bark, "Get down and give me fifty!" I couldn't help it, but I had the same feeling this morning.

"Well, we've got a little problem," she began, not removing her eyes from mine. "Darren Adler called in a little while ago. He's scheduled to work tonight with you, but it seems he's a little under the weather. Got the GI bug, he says." Her eyes narrowed for just a second or two, as she studied my response. "Anyway, he won't be coming in. Jeff has worked five nights in a row and needs a break, and Angie Weathers is going on vacation."

She paused, letting this news sink in. Staffing was the thorniest problem we had, and every once in a while it became very difficult.

We needed good people in the ER, twenty-four hours a day, especially lead nurses.

"What about Clara Adams?" I asked her, quickly glancing around to be sure she was not standing nearby. She wasn't.

"Too young and inexperienced," Virginia replied bluntly. "There's really no one else at this point."

I scratched my chin and looked down at the countertop. I was tired, ready to go home and go to bed. This problem would have to—

"What would you think about working with Patsy Wilson tonight?" Virginia asked, shifting a little and peering closer at me.

"Patsy Wilson…" I repeated slowly, the name bringing to mind a lot of memories. "Do you think she's ready?" I asked her. "I mean, it's been a couple of years, but—"

"Just got off the phone with her," she interrupted. "She's been working in a doctor's office in Pineville and is off for the next few days. She wants to give it a try. Just tonight."

"Wow, I never would have thought that," I said softly, a lot of different emotions swirling in my head and coloring my thoughts.

"Sure," I finally answered, standing straighter and taking a deep breath. "Patsy's a good nurse, and if she…if you think she'd be okay, that's fine with me."

"I think it's time," Virginia said with finality, then turned and walked toward her office.

I stood there for a moment, still scratching my chin, and thinking. Patsy Wilson had been one of the best nurses to ever work at Rock Hill General. She had grown up here in town and then got her nursing degree in Chapel Hill. She had spent some time in the CCU before coming to the ER, where she'd quickly become one of the shift charge nurses.

She was married, had two small boys, and had seemed to know every patient who came into the department. And just like Lori Davidson, she'd been calm in every circumstance, level-headed, and unshakable. That had all changed one early spring morning.

8:10 a.m. "Rock Hill ER, this is EMS 3." I was walking up the hallway from the ENT room and heard the radio squawk to life. Amy Connors quickly reached over and picked up the receiver.

"This is the ER, EMS 3," she spoke calmly, sliding a pad of paper toward her and clicking her ballpoint pen. "Whatcha got?" She had switched off the speakerphone and was listening intently.

Patsy Wilson walked over and stood behind her, glancing down as Amy made notes on the pad in front of her.

40? yr old M—cardiac arrest—tubed—no pulse

That was all Patsy needed. She looked up at me and motioned to the cardiac room.

"Cardiac arrest," she said calmly. "And a young guy, only forty or so."

Amy hung up the receiver and looked up at us. "Three minutes out," she said. "I'll call respiratory and X-ray."

"That *is* young," I muttered. That was pretty close to my own age. Too close. We would need more information about this one.

I tossed the chart of the ten-year-old with tonsillitis onto the counter as we stepped across the hallway.

"ENT needs a strep screen," I called over my shoulder to Amy.

Patsy quickly went to work in the cardiac room, opening an airway tray, just to be sure, and readying some IV fluids. Then she rolled the crash cart to the head of the stretcher, broke the seal, and opened the top drawer. The drugs we would need immediately were now accessible.

"That sounded like Denton Roberts on the radio," she said to me, not pausing from her preparations. "Glad to hear that," she added.

Denton was one of our most experienced paramedics, and we both knew this unknown and unfortunate man was in good hands.

Denton had said he'd already secured the patient's airway with an endotracheal tube, but I found myself routinely checking the light on our laryngoscope, just to be sure. Then quickly glancing around the room, I was satisfied we were ready.

A couple of minutes later, we heard the automatic ambulance entrance doors open and then the clicking of the EMS stretcher wheels as Denton and his partner made their way toward us.

Denton pulled the stretcher into cardiac with one hand while methodically bagging his patient with the other. His partner was walking beside the stretcher, performing chest compressions. Patsy hurried over to his side and guided them to the cardiac bed.

The EMS monitor was on the foot of their stretcher, and I glanced down at the small screen. Nothing—just some undulating waves that moved with the chest compressions.

"Have you had anything?" I asked as we all helped move the man to our stretcher. It was awkward, and it took a moment to get him situated where we wanted him. Whoever coined the term "dead weight" knew what they were talking about.

"Just some agonal respirations when we got to the scene," Denton answered, a little out of breath. "Nothing on the monitor. Never had a pulse. We've gone through the flatline algorithm a couple of times, but still no response."

I looked down at the dusky face of this young man, then reached out and put my fingers over his left carotid artery. There was a faint pulse, keeping time with the chest compressions being delivered by the other paramedic.

"Hold it a second, Ben," I told him.

He took a deep breath, stood up straight, gratefully put his hands on his hips, and waited.

I kept my fingers where I had placed them, feeling for any kind of pulse, any kind of cardiac activity. Nothing.

"Let's go again, Ben," I told him "Are you okay?"

"I'm fine," he answered, resuming his position near the stretcher and carefully placing his hands on the man's chest. Then once more he began his rhythmic downward thrusts.

Patsy had correctly anticipated the sequences of drugs we would use, and I listened to each side of the patient's chest, making sure he was being adequately ventilated. Textbook.

"Any idea about this guy?" I asked Denton.

"Nope. We found him slumped over in his car. Looks like he just barely made it into the parking lot of the Y. Probably going to exercise, by the looks of his clothes."

For the first time, I noticed his jogging suit and running shoes. His top had been cut open, exposing his chest. Maybe that's why I hadn't paid much attention to his attire when he first came in.

"Are you sure he was on his the way *into* the Y?" I asked Denton. "Maybe he was working out and—"

"No," he interrupted. "His car was barely pulled into the parking lot and stopped at a funny angle—like he knew he was having trouble and was trying to get off the street and out of the way. And his clothes weren't sweaty."

I reached down and felt the torn T-shirt. It was dry, and Denton was probably right. It didn't make any difference at this point, though. He wasn't responding to any of our efforts, and I was about ready to call the code. Still, I wanted to make some sense of this and figure it out if we could. If he had been working out and developed chest pain, then tried to make it to the hospital, I could understand that. But why wouldn't he have asked for help in the Y? That would have been the logical thing to do. No, I thought, Denton had it right. He was on his way to exercise and must have had a heart attack, or maybe a stroke.

"Anything else, Dr. Lesslie?" Patsy asked.

I looked up at the clock on the wall. We had been working on this man for more than forty-five minutes, and there was still no response.

"Anybody with him?" I asked the two paramedics. "Any family members or friends?"

Ben looked over and without missing a compression said, "No ID that we could find. We didn't have time to check the glove compartment of the car or anything like that, so we don't know who he is."

Patsy stepped to the head of the stretcher and looked up at Denton. "Here," she said, reaching with both hands for the ambu bag. "Let me do that for a while. Why don't you give Ben a break." Then she looked over at me, obviously wondering how long *a while* was going to be.

This guy was young and appeared to be healthy. I was reluctant to give up on him, but it was time.

"I'm fine," Ben told Patsy. Then to his partner: "Why don't you check his pockets? Maybe there's something there."

As Denton moved around the stretcher and began searching the man's pockets, I asked him, "Who called this in?" I had just thought of that. Maybe someone at the Y knew this man and had followed the ambulance to the hospital. Maybe they were out in the waiting room right now.

"Don't know that one," he answered, now leaning over the man and reaching into the back pocket of his sweatpants. "You'll have to check with dispatch. When we got there, a few cars were parked out in front, but there was nobody around. We just got going and didn't have time to check it out."

He was about to stand up, when he leaned over a little farther and said, "Wait, here's something."

He fished a small leather wallet out of the man's pocket, then held it up for us to see. "Let me check this out," he said, stepping over to the counter behind the head of the stretcher and opening the wallet.

I looked up at the clock once more and was about to call the code, when Denton exclaimed, "Well, look at this!"

He was studying a small card of some kind, flipping it back and forth to get better light on its shiny surface. "Looks like he's got some kind of surgical problem, or something," he mused.

"What do you mean?" I asked, puzzled by this new information. Maybe there was some clue here, some unrevealed pathology that might guide us in this man's care. Maybe there was something we were missing.

"Yeah, it looks like he has an appointment with Stuart Lowry. At least, that's the name on the card."

Stuart Lowry—"Stu" to everyone on the hospital staff—was a general surgeon in town. He was a great guy—funny, easygoing, always cheerful. And he never minded coming to the ER when we needed him.

"Is there any diagnosis on the card, or any reason for his appointment?" I asked Denton. "Sometimes they'll have that on there."

He looked at the front and back of the card once again. Suddenly he looked up at me, wide-eyed and pale. "Doc," he stammered. "This is an ID card."

I was stunned and for a split second just stared at him, trying to understand what he had just said.

"It's what?" I whispered.

"Oh my Lord!"

It was Patsy Wilson, and she was looking down at the face of the man on the stretcher.

She took a step back from the bed and cried out, "It's Stu Lowry."

It couldn't be. This was impossible.

I looked down now, studying the features of this man lying before us. Flat on his back, his facial muscles now slack, and with a tube in his mouth and oxygen prongs in his nose. It was easy to understand why no one had recognized him. But it *was* Stu. There was no doubt about that.

But nothing had changed. We were still not getting any response, and though we worked with him for another twenty minutes, it was only becoming more obvious. He was gone.

"Let's call it," I sadly told the people in the room.

I held a Code Blue clipboard in my hand, waiting for Patsy to give me the official time so I could write it down. When she didn't say anything, I looked over in her direction. She was staring down at Stu, unblinking, and not moving.

Denton looked over at her and then at the clock by the head of the stretcher, which was just out of my sight.

"9:12," he told me, reaching out and putting a hand on Patsy's shoulder.

"Come on," he gently told her. "Let's go."

Later that morning, I stepped into Virginia Granger's office.

"Have you seen Patsy?" I asked her.

She looked up from her desk and said, "I sent her home. She's pretty upset about Dr. Lowry."

Then she told me why.

Stu and Patsy had grown up together in Rock Hill, had attended the same elementary and high schools, and had even dated before they had gone off to different colleges. They had managed to remain close friends, and now their children played together, and they and their families all went to the same church.

"This is really quite a blow for her," Virginia said quietly, slowly shaking her head. "I don't think I've ever seen her so upset. That's why I sent her home."

That was the last shift Patsy Wilson had worked in the ER. She hadn't been able to get over the shock of that morning and the loss of her friend.

And now she was going to be working with me tonight. That would be good, but maybe a little strained and awkward. Maybe more than a little.

But by the time I got home and into the shower, I knew the good would outweigh any of the negatives, and I was looking forward to her return.

6

When Angels Cry

6:58 p.m. The ER parking lot was full and there were three ambulances stacked up at the emergency entrance. Not a good omen for what lay in wait for me behind those doors.

It was like stepping into a frenzied nightclub. People were moving around everywhere, and the noise was chaotic, the voices incoherent.

"Excuse me, Dr. Lesslie!" someone called out just to my right. It was one of our techs, and she was trying to push the EKG machine down the crowded hallway.

I quickly moved out of her way and thought about stepping outside. Maybe if I closed my eyes, counted to three, and came back in... No, that never seemed to work.

Amy Connors caught my eye from behind the nurses' station. She shook her head and silently mouthed, "I'm outta here." Then she stood up and made her way to the lounge to pick up her things and head home.

Liz Kennick was standing at the counter, writing on a chart. She looked up as I approached her.

"It has been absolutely crazy!" she said in understatement. "Just look at this place," she added, her right hand sweeping around the department for effect.

"Don't worry, Liz," I told her. "It happens."

Then setting my briefcase on the floor, I asked, "Have you got anything to turn over to me?"

Just then, a stretcher came out of major trauma, guided by two paramedics. There was a bundle of clothes on its foot, along with a large, stuffed-full folder, the kind we used for medical records. The twentysomething young man lying there was being transferred out of the department, and when the paramedics came up beside the nurses' station, they stopped.

"Have we got everything we need?" one of them asked Liz.

She spun around, looked down at the young man, and said, "He's ready to go. They'll be expecting him in the ER at CMC. Good luck, Mr. Tucker," she added, patting the man on his left arm.

"Thanks, Doc," he replied, smiling up at her.

I took a good look at him as he lay there before me. He seemed to be in no distress, with normal color and what seemed like a normal neurological response. The only significant thing I noted was a large bandage wrapped around his head, covering an odd horn-like shape sticking up from the top of his skull. I wondered why he was being sent out to a trauma center.

The paramedics wheeled him toward the ambulance entrance and Liz suddenly put her pen on the counter and looked up at me.

"Come over here, Robert," she told me. "I want you to see something."

She quickly stepped over to the X-ray view box and I followed.

"Take a look at this!" she said, flipping on the light and illuminating the film that was hanging there.

Wow—now that was something! It was the lateral view of the skull of an adult—nothing unusual in and of itself. What *was* unusual was the large nail driven through the top of this person's head—half on the outside of the skull, and half in the brain.

I glanced at the closing ambulance entrance doors, now understanding the pointed bandage on the top of that young man's head. But he had been wide awake, and acting as if there was no problem.

"What happened?" I asked Liz while looking at some of his other X-rays. It seemed that the nail went right into the middle of the top of his brain.

"Nail-gun accident," she said matter-of-factly, as if she had seen hundreds of these in her short career. "He was working on a construction site, downstairs, minding his own business, when someone on the floor above him fired his gun into some plywood. The nail went all the way through the floor, hit him in the head, and knocked him down. But he never lost consciousness. It's amazing, but he's completely intact. No deficit that I can find. But that nail has to be sitting in his brain. We started some antibiotics and called one of the neurosurgeons in Charlotte. He's going to see him up there in the ER. Should do okay."

"Wow," I remarked as we walked back to the nurses' station. "I've never seen anything like that before."

Answering my earlier question, Liz said, "There's only one patient I need to leave you with, Robert. There's a two- or three-year-old in 4. Minor head trauma. He fell and hit the back of his skull about dinnertime, and is around in CT now. Shouldn't be much longer. No loss of consciousness, but he's got a big goose egg there, and his parents think he's not acting quite right. Anyway, should be negative, and he should be able to go home."

With that, she closed the chart in front of her, tossed it into the discharge box, and with one hand slapped the top of the counter.

"And I'm gone," she said, smiling. Then glancing around the department, she added, "Good luck."

From across the room, the door to Virginia Granger's office opened, and out she walked. I looked up at the clock on the wall, a little confused. She was here every day during the week, but usually left around five o'clock. What was she doing here now?

A few steps behind her walked Darren Adler, dressed and apparently ready for work. Virginia saw me and started over in my direction.

When the two stood in front of me at the nurses' station, I was better able to see Darren's face. He was a pale green, and the corners of his mouth were turned down. Looking closer, I noticed some small beads of sweat on his forehead. He was sick, and obviously didn't feel too well.

"Darren called earlier this afternoon," Virginia began to tell me. "He said he was feeling a little better and wants to try to work." She paused and looked doubtfully over at the nurse. "I'm not so sure, but he's insisting he's okay."

"Darren, you don't look so good," I told him honestly. "We've got someone else to work for you tonight, and it won't—"

"I'm fine, Dr. Lesslie," he said, trying unsuccessfully to muster a little bravado. "Things turned the corner around noon, and I haven't had any more vomiting since then. I really want to work, and I'll... I'll be fine."

I looked over at Virginia for some help. She raised her eyebrows, pursed her lips, but didn't say anything.

"What about Patsy Wilson?" I asked her, hoping that she might have already come in.

"I explained things to her, and she's sort of on standby. She understands—and if we don't need her tonight, she still wants to try working sometime."

I studied Darren's face again and thought about the state of the department. It was going to be tough for him, but I knew he was on thin ice. And I knew Virginia was leaving the decision up to me.

"Do you think you can handle it?" I asked him.

"I can do it, Doc."

I looked at him for another moment and then, with some trepidation, relented. After all, Patsy Wilson was out there if we needed her.

"Okay, Darren. Get going then."

"Thanks, Doc," he said, mustering a smile. "And thanks, Ms. Granger."

He turned and walked toward the nurses' station. I was about to follow him when Virginia said, "Dr. Lesslie, I need to speak with you for a moment."

It was not a request. She turned and walked back into her office, and I followed, closing the door behind me.

"I know you need to get out there," she began. "But this will only take a moment. You need to know that we have a problem with our medications."

I already knew about the Vistaril business. Now what?

"The narcotics count has been off twice this week," she calmly explained. "We're missing four vials of Demerol."

"What? Are you sure?"

"You know the procedure, and yes, I'm sure," she answered flatly.

At the beginning and ending of each shift, two of our nurses would go through the narcotics cabinet, counting each unit of each drug, making sure that what was in the cabinet matched what was in our log. It was a state and federal requirement, and something we took very seriously.

"How does something like that happen?" I asked her, my mind turning on recent events and possibilities.

"On Monday there was one missing," she explained. "And Lori Davidson brought it to my attention. We've had that happen occasionally in the past, and it usually shakes out in a couple of days. Once the pharmacy made a mistake in their count, and another time the pharmacist found the missing vials stored in another location. I was hoping that would be the case this time, since there was just one vial unaccounted for. But this morning, three more turned up missing. We've looked everywhere, but nothing so far. I just wanted to make you aware, and ask that you keep your eyes open for any unusual activity or behavior. I've notified the administration, and they will have to start their own investigation."

Great! I thought. *That's all we need, someone from admin poking around the department, creating a stir and solving nothing.*

"I'll do that, Virginia," I told her, dispirited by this development. "I hope it turns out to be something simple."

"I don't believe it will, Robert."

Virginia left the department, and as the shift wore on, Darren Adler's color improved and he seemed to be getting stronger. It looked like he would be fine.

"Dr. Lesslie, the CT scan on the kid in room 4 is back," the unit secretary told me, not looking up from her work.

I had forgotten about the child. It had taken longer to get his scan done than Liz had anticipated. It was almost nine o'clock when I went into the room with the radiologist's report in my hand.

Glancing down quickly at the name on the chart I said, "This must be Clark." I walked over to the stretcher where the three-year-old boy was quietly sitting. He looked up at me as I said his name, but didn't smile. He gave a quick, furtive glance at his parents, and then he looked down again at his hands.

Odd, I thought. And it was a little odd that he was sitting alone on the bed, his feet dangling over the edge, bare-chested.

I looked over in the corner of the room. A young woman, his mother I presumed, was sitting on the lone stool. She looked over at me and smiled. The man beside her stood with his arms folded across his chest, scowling.

"This has certainly taken long enough," he muttered, looking down at the small child.

"And you are…?" I questioned them.

"We're his parents, Lewis and Erica Springs," he told me bluntly. "Tell us about the CT so we can get home."

He still hadn't looked at me, and I studied him for a moment. He was probably in his mid-thirties, dressed in a starched shirt and bright red tie, and wearing expensive shoes. His wife, Erica, was neatly dressed as well, and sat with her hands politely folded in her lap. She had glanced up at her husband when he said this, and then turned her head away.

I turned my attention back to Clark.

"Tell me, son, what happened to you today?" I asked him, stepping over and sitting down beside him on the stretcher. Without looking up, he quickly slid a few inches away from me.

"We've already gone over this," Lewis Springs interjected. "With that other doctor, the woman."

"Lewis, please…" his wife implored. "Let him—"

"She wrote everything down on that chart," he cut her off, his voice now raised a little. "Just tell us about the scan."

"Before we go over that," I said, looking over at the two of them, "I need to know exactly what happened."

Lewis exhaled loudly and turned a little, facing away from me.

"He was just running through the house this evening," Erica explained. "He must have tripped and fallen and hit his head. As I told Dr. Kennick—I believe that's her name—he didn't get knocked out, but he quickly got a big hematoma on the back of his head, and he vomited once. We were just concerned and wanted him checked out."

"I understand," I told her, looking now at Clark. Gently, I felt the back of his head and the large swelling there. I couldn't feel any bony defect, and there was no active bleeding. I knew the scan was negative, but I wanted to be sure he was okay.

"Has he complained of pain anywhere else?" I asked her, now focusing my attention on his wrists and shoulders. Those areas were frequently injured when a child, or anyone else for that matter, took a tumble.

"No, just the back of his head," she answered. "Everything else seems fine. I took a good look at him too."

Lewis was tapping his foot now, becoming more impatient.

Things weren't quite right here. Nobody liked being in the ER and having to wait a long time. But this was their child, and they should want to be sure he was all right, no matter how long it took. Their behavior didn't quite fit the circumstances, and Clark seemed sullen, almost withdrawn. Something was bothering me.

Suddenly, there it was.

"Mrs. Springs, you said he was running through the house this afternoon?" I asked her.

"Yes, he was…just like he always does. He was running and must have tripped on something."

She had hesitated, just for a split second—but she had hesitated.

That's what didn't make sense. Children his age lead with their faces when they fall. We see busted lips and chins and eyebrows. Not the backs of heads. Why would he have fallen backward? Maybe his feet had gone out from under him, but that didn't happen very often.

I leaned back a little on the stretcher and looked again at the back of his head. Then I looked at his chest and lower back. There were subtle areas of bruising, and what looked like a few small welts.

"Mrs. Springs," I said, glancing over at her. "Tell me about these areas. Did he do this when he fell this evening?"

Erica quickly glanced up at her husband before standing and moving toward the stretcher. She put a hand on her boy's shoulder and looked at this back.

"Yes…he must have….he must have done this at the same time," she murmured. "I saw that too, but it doesn't look too bad, does it?"

I gently ran my fingers over a few of the bruises, and Clark winced a little and pulled away. But he didn't say anything or cry out.

"We need to take a look at this too, then," I told them. "I'm going to send him around for a chest X-ray, just to be sure there's no problem with his lungs or anything."

I wasn't very worried about *these* bruises. I was more interested in finding out whether Clark had any old fractures anywhere. I was becoming increasingly concerned about his safety.

"Just tell us about the CT scan," Lewis said, stepping into the middle of the room. "We'll take him to his pediatrician in the morning and have his back checked out."

I looked down at the radiology report and then up into the faces of Lewis and Erica Clark.

"His CT scan is fine," I told them. "There's no skull fracture, and no bleeding or anything going on in his head."

"Good," Lewis said with determination. "Then we'll be on our way."

He reached out and took hold of his son's right arm. The boy jerked away and looked up at his mother with wide and frightened eyes. She didn't move.

"I'm afraid we're not quite ready to release him," I told Lewis Springs, standing up and positioning myself in front of the boy.

"*Release* him?" Lewis sneered. "And just who are *you* to release my son? Come on, Erica, we're leaving."

He was beginning to pull on his son's arm, and for the first time Clark whimpered.

Leaning closer to the frightened child, I said, "Mr. Lewis, I can't let you do that."

He dropped the boy's arm and put his finger in my face. His own face had turned deep red and he was sputtering in anger.

"Do you know who I am?" he demanded. "I will have your license, Dr. Lesslie. I am personal friends with the hospital administrator, and tomorrow morning, you will not have a job. Now get out of our way! We're going home!"

I didn't move, surprised a little at my own composure. But this wasn't about me. It was about Clark Springs.

"Here's what's going to happen tonight, Mr. Springs," I told him calmly, disregarding the finger just inches from my nose. "We're going to get those X-rays, and then I'm going to get a stat consult from DSS. There are too many red flags here for me to feel comfortable with Clark's safety."

Erica's head slumped to her chest and she moved back a little from her husband.

"You're going to what!" he yelled. "I'm warning you, you—"

"Just a second," I interrupted him, stepping toward the entrance of the room and pulling aside the curtain.

"Susan," I called out to the unit secretary. She looked over in my direction and I said loudly, "Call the police. We need them right now."

I stepped back into the room and pulled the curtain closed.

"Now, Mr. Springs, what happens at this point is completely up to you."

He glared at me, his fists clenched and his eyes mere slits. I knew at that moment anything could happen. And I just waited.

"Lewis," his wife whispered, reaching out and touching his arm.

He jerked away from her, was about to say something to me, then stomped out of the room. Clark just sat there, seemingly oblivious to all that had just transpired.

The radiologist and I looked carefully at Clark's X-rays. It was awful. There were three healing rib fractures on the left side of his chest and two more on the right. Kids just don't break their ribs unless there is some major form of trauma. Like their other bones, their ribs usually bend before snapping.

"Take a look at this," the radiologist said, pointing to Clark's right upper arm. There was a healing fracture there as well, probably only three or four weeks old. "Takes a lot of force to do that," he muttered angrily.

I just stood there, looking over his shoulder and shaking my head.

"I don't know how you folks in the ER deal with this stuff," he said quietly. "I'm just looking at the films here, but you've got the child right in front of you. It must be hard not getting upset and really angry."

It *was* hard. And it was heartbreaking. I thought of the quote Lori Davidson had taped to the inside of her locker. I had seen it only once, but I would never forget it:

> *Let my heart be broken*
> *with the things*
> *that break the heart of God.*

Something like this would always break our hearts.

"Do you know who this guy is?" he asked me, spinning around in his chair and taking off his bifocals.

"No," I answered. "And I don't really care."

"He's a big shot in town," he informed me. "Works with some financial group in Charlotte, I think. And he used to be on the board of the hospital."

"Well, that should be interesting," I remarked. "Thanks for your help here," I added, walking toward the doorway.

"Good luck, Robert," he said quietly.

I stopped and turned to face him. "It's the little boy who needs the good luck. So far, he hasn't had very much."

Hopefully that would be changing for Clark Springs. And hopefully Lewis Springs's troubles were just beginning.

When I got back to the ER, two police officers were stepping into room 4.

I was physically and emotionally drained when the ambulance doors opened and my relief walked through them. And I was more than happy to see Ted Nivens, one of my partners, as he walked over to me, smiling.

"Let's get you out of here, Robert," he said, looking around the department. "Anything I can do?"

We had somehow managed to empty it out, and I had no one to turn over to him.

Darren Adler sat on the other side of the counter, exhausted as well, but managing somehow to nod his head in agreement.

"Nope, Ted," I said to him. "Everything's done. It's all yours."

Then looking down at my nurse: "Darren, you did a great job tonight. I'm not sure I could have done it, looking the way you did when you came in. But good job."

"Thanks, Doc," he said weakly, smiling up at me. "And thanks for giving me the chance."

7

The Witching Hour

8:40 p.m. This was my last night for a while, and I was looking forward to a couple of days off. It was Thursday, one of our quieter days, and the department was reasonably under control. That could always change quickly, but for the moment, we were enjoying the relative calm.

Jeff Ryan walked through the triage door leading a young woman. He gave me his "I don't have a clue!" look as he passed the nurses' station and took her to room 5. I caught a glimpse of her face as she came by, as did our secretary, Susan Everett.

"What in the world!" she whispered, her eyes glued on the patient until she disappeared behind the curtain. "Did you see that, Dr. Lesslie?"

"I did," I answered, wondering what was going on. "Pretty impressive."

The woman's face was a glowing, brightly colored beet-red. No, it was more of a fire-engine red. She didn't seem to be in any distress, and I waited curiously for Jeff to come out of the room and give us her story.

He pulled the curtain closed behind him, then walked over. Sliding the chart of room 5 over in front of me, he said, "This beats all, Doc. She looks like a lobster, a boiled one, and she's giving off heat like one too."

I looked down at the chart.

Dakota Flanders—22 yr old F—hot flashes

It was a descriptive complaint, but it didn't help me very much.

"Odd name," I remarked to Jeff.

"Yeah, she's a student at Winthrop, from out West somewhere. Says she and a couple of her friends went out to dinner, and when she got back to the dorm, she felt a little flushed. One of her friends checked on her and got all excited. They almost called an ambulance but decided to drive over here instead. All of her vital signs are fine, and she's breathing okay. Just looks like she's been cooked."

"That's interesting," I said thoughtfully, picking up the chart and walking over to Dakota's room.

She was sitting on the stretcher, her legs hanging over the edge, and she looked up and smiled when I entered the room.

"Miss Flanders," I said, walking over to a stool and sitting down. "I'm Dr. Lesslie. Tell me what's going on tonight."

She calmly repeated what she had told Jeff in triage, then asked me what I thought was happening to her.

"Where did you have dinner?" I questioned her.

"Captain's Quarters," she answered, naming a chain seafood restaurant on Cherry Road. "We go there every once in a while but have never had any problems. And I'm not allergic to anything, no shellfish or stuff like that."

"Do you remember what you had?" I persisted, beginning to think this might be the answer.

"Sure," she said without hesitation. "I had the special—grilled mahi-mahi. But I've had that before, and I've always been fine. Why? Could that have caused this?"

"Maybe," I told her. "Do you remember how it tasted? Was there something different about it?"

"No, not different," she answered, putting her index finger on the side of her face, thinking hard. "It was blackened this time, and pretty spicy. But not different."

That was it. I had been down this path myself once. Some blackened tuna from one of the local restaurants had done me in. The peppery flavor should have tipped me off, but I had been hungry and in a hurry, and had eaten the whole serving. Within twenty minutes, I was lighting up like a Christmas tree.

It's called scombroid poisoning, and it happens often enough that not only had I had it myself, but I had seen several cases of it in the ER. It's caused by a bacterium that forms a toxin on improperly prepared and stored fish. The toxin resembles histamine, thus the allergic-type reaction we see. The extent of the reaction and flushing is dose-dependent, and by the looks of Dakota, she had gotten a pretty good dose. Just like me.

"We're going to give you some Benadryl," I told her. "And if it's what I think it is, you should be a lot better in fifteen or twenty minutes."

Jeff walked out of room 5, having given Dakota her injection of Benadryl fifteen minutes earlier.

"She's doing great, Doc," he said, walking over to where I stood. "Almost back to normal and ready to go home."

I had explained the poisoning to Jeff and Susan and told them the young college student should do fine, with no further problems. I was about to tell them about my personal experience with this, when I suddenly remembered the rest of the story. At the time, I had looked up the condition in a medical textbook to make sure I wasn't going to die. It sounded straightforward until I came upon a very troubling statement.

One to two hours after the onset of symptoms, the patient will develop abdominal cramps and profuse diarrhea.

It had been uncanny. As I had closed the book, my stomach had begun to rumble, and then—

"Hello, nurse?"

It was Dakota Flanders, peering out from behind the curtain of room 5, her voice sounding strained.

"Is there a bathroom nearby?"

3:05 a.m.—the witching hour. We had made it to the time of night when anything might come through those ambulance doors or through triage. Clara Adams had been right the other day when she had said the patients who came to the ER in the middle of the night could be very "interesting."

Jeff had discharged our only remaining patient and we were sitting at the nurses' station with Susan. The buzzer from the business office fired off, indicating there was a new patient out front.

Having just sat down, Jeff grumbled something unintelligible, pushed back his chair, got up, and ambled out to triage.

A few minutes later, the door to triage opened and he walked back into the department leading Lucinda Banks. When I saw who it was, my heart sank.

Lucinda was a fifty-year-old accountant, and this morning she was dressed as usual, wearing a neatly tailored business suit and high heels. Jeff rolled his eyes at me as they passed the counter and headed toward room 4. Lucinda's eyes remained intently focused on the back of her nurse's head.

Lucinda Banks would have made Baron Munchhausen proud. Of course, he should be proud of *himself.* After all, how many people had a "syndrome" named after them? Munchausen's Syndrome (somebody dropped one of the H's over the past century or so) describes those individuals who make up fantastic, exotic, and totally untrue stories about themselves. In the baron's case, he was apparently trying to impress his friends and acquaintances with tales of daring and adventure. With those suffering from the syndrome, the intent is totally different. Their goal is to convince their health-care giver that they have a significant and sometimes life-threatening illness, their ultimate objective being admission to the hospital.

Early in my career, I just didn't believe this syndrome really existed. It seemed too far-fetched. These individuals were apparently willing to undergo all manner of testing, poking, and prodding—at times quite painful—just to be believed and admitted. It just didn't make any sense to me, and I couldn't comprehend it. I was convinced it was an illness concocted for a magazine article or a TV show—until I met Lucinda.

The first time I had met her had been in the ER about two years ago. She had come in during the middle of the night, just like tonight, and complained of shortness of breath. The triage nurse was concerned enough to put her in the cardiac room and then immediately came to find me.

Lucinda was complaining of right-sided chest pain, shortness of breath, right calf pain, and an episode of nearly blacking out. Her vital signs had all been stable, her oxygen saturation was normal, and clinically she looked fine. The problem was that all of her symptoms pointed to her having a pulmonary embolus—a blood clot in her lung. She was a classic presentation. Her reaction to this news was a little peculiar, though. She had almost smiled when I told her and seemed almost happy I had come to this conclusion. I explained that we would need to do some further testing, including a blood gas, which was a painful procedure. It involves a needle puncture of the radial artery at the wrist, and then aspiration of a small amount of arterial blood. It hurts, and it's not anything I would want to have done unless absolutely necessary. But it was part of the workup for Lucinda and would provide additional support for this diagnosis.

She would also need a lung scan, as well as additional blood work and an ultrasound of her right leg.

"Sounds like I'll need to be in the hospital," she had remarked, strangely calm and seeming to be almost relieved at this turn of events. This was a life-threatening problem, and I had done my best to explain the seriousness of her condition to her. Maybe I wasn't communicating very well.

A couple of hours later, I had the results of all of her studies in front of me. Everything was completely normal. Now what?

As I explained these findings to her, her face seemed to cloud over, and she became a little agitated. I had expected her to be happy that things were pointing away from an embolus.

"Oooh!" she began moaning, clutching her right chest. "I can't breathe!"

She was gasping, and I was just standing there looking down at her, when one of our nurses hurried into the room. She had heard the moaning from out in the hallway.

"Dr. Lesslie, is there anything we need to do?" she had asked me anxiously.

At that point, I had given up. I talked the pulmonary specialist on call into putting her in the hospital with a diagnosis of "possible pulmonary embolus" and then seeing how things would shake out over the next few days. When I saw him in the ER later on that week, he told me he had sent Lucinda home the next morning.

"I still don't know what's going on with her," he had told me. "All of her studies stayed normal, and she never ran any fever or had any abnormal vital signs. She didn't want to leave the hospital, but I told her she had to be discharged. We weren't doing anything for her here except providing a bed and three meals a day."

He *had* learned a few things from her family doctor, though. She had reported a history of cancer (not true), a recent five-hour plane flight (also not true), and a distant family history of an unusual bleeding problem (how could you ever confirm that?).

"She seemed to know all the risk factors for an embolus, and she had all of the symptoms. And you know what, Robert? It's almost as if she wanted to have one. That's what beats me."

I hadn't felt so bad when I learned she had stumped one of our best pulmonary guys. But Lucinda Banks was puzzling—something I had never run into before.

The next time I saw her was a few days after Thanksgiving, about a year later. On this occasion she came to the ER in the middle of the afternoon, dressed the same way as before—very professional and very polished.

She had all the classic symptoms of a heart attack, but with none of the physical or laboratory findings. One of our cardiologists reluctantly put her in the hospital and, as expected, everything turned up normal. She even had a negative heart cath.

When I saw the cardiologist a few days later, we talked about Lucinda. He mentioned the idea of Munchausen's and wondered if that might be what was going on with this woman.

When I got the chance, I looked up this strange malady. The more I read about it, the more it seemed to fit. In fact, it perfectly described Lucinda and explained all of her behavior, all of her lack of objective findings, and all of her expert knowledge of her disease du jour.

We hadn't seen Lucinda again after that chest pain visit, not until tonight. I was curious about what her complaint was going to be this time. Based on Jeff's reaction, it must be something interesting.

He walked out of her room and over to the nurses' station.

"Good luck with this," he whispered, handing me the chart and glancing back over his shoulder. "I can't make heads nor tails of it."

The buzzer had gone off again and he headed back out to triage.

He had written *multiple complaints—headache, visual changes, kidney failure*—on Lucinda's ER record.

Kidney failure? I thought. *Now that's something different. How did she come up with that one?*

Another quick glance at her chart informed me that her blood pressure was normal, as were her pulse and temperature. Again.

"Ms. Banks," I said to her as I stepped into room 4. "I'm Dr. Lesslie. What can we do for you tonight?"

"I remember you, Dr. Lesslie," she replied pleasantly, looking up at me and smoothing the stretcher sheet on either side of her. She was sitting up with her legs dangling from the edge of the bed, crossed at her ankles.

"I'm just not sure what's wrong with me," she sighed, slowly shaking her head and folding her hands in her lap. "I started having this strange numbness in my hands, and then in my feet. And I've noticed that my vision isn't what it should be."

She paused and rubbed her eyes, struggling to focus on some object off in the corner of the room.

"And then all my joints started to hurt, especially my wrists and fingers and hips. I feel like I've been run over by a truck!"

She looked up at me, waiting for a response. I just stood there, nodded my head, and waited for her to go on.

After a moment, she continued. "And these headaches—they're awful! Right here at my temples." She was rubbing the sides of her head now, wincing in terrible pain.

She didn't say anything further, and this time I couldn't wait her out. I finally asked her, "Tell me about this kidney failure. Who diagnosed that, and when did it start?"

She seemed relieved that we were finally moving down her list of complaints, and she stopped rubbing her head. She looked up at me and sighed.

"My family doctor was worried it would only be a matter of time," she informed me. "My urine output has been diminishing over the past few months, and now, my kidneys seem to have shut down completely."

She said this with a surety and calmness that rattled me a little. This was a bright woman, and I was having a hard time believing what I was hearing.

I glanced down at her vital signs again. Most people with kidney failure had an elevated blood pressure. Lucinda's was 110/78. And her pulse was 70.

"I haven't been able to produce any urine in more than 24 hours," she told me, searching my eyes for the hoped-for alarm.

I was tempted to have one of the nurses put in a Foley catheter and call her out on this, but something told me that wasn't the way to handle this. That's probably what she wanted me to do, as well as get a bunch of lab work. Instead, I just stood there, holding her chart, and meeting her gaze with mine.

There was a split second where I thought I saw the corners of her mouth turn down. Then there was that smile again, almost condescending. But she was beginning to lose her patience. I wasn't jumping down this rabbit hole quickly enough.

"Do you...do you think I could have lupus?" she asked with feigned trepidation.

"Hmm..." I responded, and started stroking my chin, seemingly struck by this surprising possibility.

Of course it sounded like lupus. She was describing all of the symptoms of this disease, even stretching things to the point of manufacturing the findings of one of the disease's end-stage complications— kidney failure. But that one was going to be hard for her to validate. Yet...what was the best way to handle this? We had already put her in the hospital twice for imagined maladies, and that was just at Rock Hill General. Who knew how many other places she had been with these complaints? And who knew how many other diseases there were whose symptoms she had manufactured?

"Dr. Lesslie, do you think lupus could explain this?"

She leaned toward me, turning one side of her face for me to examine.

I hadn't noticed it before in the less than optimal lighting of the exam room, but as she came closer, I could see that her cheeks and forehead were obviously a little more flushed than the rest of her face. It was the classic "butterfly" distribution of the facial rash of lupus—the "red wolf." She had really done her reading.

But how had she managed to do this? The rash *was* in the typically described form and was the appropriate color. I looked closer. It was all I could do not to say something, but there was the answer. It was clear that Lucinda had applied a faint dusting of makeup to her cheeks and forehead. It was very subtle, but it was definitely makeup.

That was enough. Now I knew what I had to do.

"Lucinda, this is very concerning," I told her truthfully. "I'm going to make a few phone calls and we're going to get you some help."

Relieved at last, she leaned back on the stretcher and said, "Thank you, Dr. Lesslie. Thank you so much."

When I got to the nurses' station, I slumped into one of the chairs. Susan looked over at me, puzzled.

"Do we need to do anything for the woman in 4?" she asked.

"Would you call up to the behavioral med unit and see if one of the psych doctors is up there?" It was a long shot at this time of the morning, but we might get lucky.

A few minutes later, I was talking with Martin Childress, the on-call psychiatrist. He had happened to be upstairs handling a problem patient when Susan had called.

I told him about Lucinda Banks, hoping desperately that he might be willing to take a look at her.

When I finished describing her case, there was a long pause on the other end of the phone. I was trying to think of my next step, when Martin said, "Robert, that sounds fascinating. Let me finish up here with this patient, and I'll be down and talk with Ms. Banks. Thirty minutes okay?"

"That would be great," I said gratefully. "She'll be right here in room 4."

I hung up the phone, relieved and thankful for the help. And I was thankful that Lucinda Banks was going to get some help. She didn't have lupus, or heart disease, or a blood clot in her lungs. She needed psychiatric help and not another lengthy and futile workup.

When Martin Childress came down the hallway a little while later, I picked up the chart for room 4 and handed it to him.

"Thanks again for seeing her," I told him.

"No problem," he responded, studying the front sheet of her record. "I'll let you know what I find."

He walked over to room 4, stepped in, and pulled the curtain closed behind him. I sat there, watching and listening for some explosion, some outburst from Lucinda. But the room remained quiet.

"Here," Jeff said, sliding the chart of room 3 over to me. "Bobby Craddock. Eight-year-old with a sore throat and temp of 102."

I picked up the chart, read his name, noted the complaint and the boy's temp, and thought—*A sore throat. Thank you, Bobby Craddock.*

8

Out of Death Comes Life

Friday, 7:45 a.m. Virginia Granger had been in her office with the door closed for the past half hour. That wasn't anything unusual. What *was* unusual was that she had been meeting all this time with Walter Stevens, one of the hospital's VP's. I couldn't remember what he was VP of, but I knew he was young and hadn't been on the job for very long.

They must be discussing the department's missing medication. Nothing had turned up to explain the inconsistent narcotics count, and now the administration was involved. That certainly didn't thrill Virginia.

Her door opened and she stepped partway out.

"Dr. Lesslie," she called, getting my attention as I stepped out of the medication room. I had been washing my hands, looking out the window into the parking lot. I'd been watching a young mother herd her four young children toward the ER entrance and thinking that none of them seemed very ill. Maybe they were just visiting.

Virginia caught my eye, then motioned with her hand for me to join her.

I finished drying my hands, tossed the paper towel in the trash can at the nurses' station, and walked over to her office.

She was just sitting down behind her desk when I entered. I closed the door behind me and walked over.

"Have a seat, Robert," she said, motioning to the remaining chair in front of her desk. In the other chair sat Walter Stevens. He had on a long-sleeved white shirt and wore a bright-red bow-tie. In one of his hands was a legal pad filled with scribbled notes. When he noticed me looking down at it, he quickly flipped it over in his lap.

"Dr. Lesslie," he intoned with an air of gravity. "It's good to see you."

He held out his hand and I shook it. I was struck once again by the damp weakness of his handshake. I had met the twenty-eight-year-old when he had first arrived at Rock Hill General. He had just finished his MBA program at some small school in eastern Kentucky and had struck me then as being a little too sure of himself, and a little too smug. Nothing seemed to have changed.

"Walter, good morning," I told him, sitting down and turning to face Virginia. "What's going on?" I asked the two of them.

The head nurse put her palms down on the desk in front of her and leaned toward the two of us.

"Walter and I have been discussing the matter of the missing narcotics," she began. "And I think he may have some ideas."

There was little enthusiasm in her face, and less in her eyes.

"What makes you sure they're missing?" I asked. "I had hoped this was simply an oversight. Has there not been some simple explanation?"

"There is an explanation, to be sure," Walter intoned. "But it is not simple."

Virginia turned in her chair, reached behind her, and picked up a small box from the bookshelf behind her.

"Take a look at this," she said, sliding the plastic-wrapped container over to me.

I recognized it immediately. It was a medication container—a two-and-a-half-inch cube shrink-wrapped in plastic. It contained 25 glass vials of some type of medication, arranged neatly in five rows of five vials each. The tops of the vials were all that was visible, the rest being surrounded by a paper box. Each vial was protected from the others by a thin, cross-hatched insert. One side of the container read *Demerol—100 mg*. I turned the box over in my hands, examining each side. It looked to be brand-new and unopened.

I thought Virginia might be testing me, and I thought of something. Looking down once more, I checked the expiration date. It was still current.

Putting the box down on her desk, I said, "Looks like a box of unopened Demerol to me, Virginia. Is there something important here?"

"You didn't look quite closely enough, Dr. Lesslie," Walter Stevens said, snatching up the box of medicine and holding it in front of me. He oriented the cube so that the bottom of it was right under my nose.

The guy was starting to get on my nerves, but when I glanced over at Virginia, she gave me a brief nod of her head.

Reluctantly, I looked once more at the Demerol, this time focusing more intently on the bottom of the box. Again, it looked fine to me, with the plastic perfectly in place. There didn't seem to be any evidence of tampering, or of someone trying to open it.

Wait a minute.

"Let me hold that a second," I said to Stevens, taking the box out of his hand and moving it around in the light.

There, just to the right of dead center. I looked closer, not wanting to believe this and needing to be sure.

But there it was—a small hole, almost invisible. And there was another one, about half an inch away. And another. I counted six holes in the bottom of the box. I flipped it over and examined the vials that were sitting above these holes, looking at them closely. Just what I was afraid of—they were empty.

I lowered my hand to the desk and looked up at Virginia. She was studying my eyes, waiting for my response, waiting for me to say something.

Looking down at the Demerol again, I said, "Very clever."

Someone had taken a small needle and syringe and deftly sucked the Demerol out of six of the vials, spacing the punctures so the box still seemed balanced and full. And with a small enough needle, they wouldn't have drawn any broken glass into their syringe.

"Very clever," I mused again.

"Not clever, Dr. Lesslie," Stevens said, once again taking the box from my hand and placing it on the table. "This is *criminal.*"

Cleverly criminal, I wanted to say, having to bite my tongue to remain silent.

But he was right—this was serious business. We had a problem in the department, and it was bigger than I had thought.

"Have we checked the other medications?" I asked Virginia, fearing the worst.

"It seems this is the first one," she answered quietly. "No other evidence of any tampering. But whoever did this has an intensity of purpose and will likely go to extremes to get what they're after."

"And we've narrowed our list of possible suspects to just a few people," Walter added, leaning back in the chair and bridging his fingers, spiderlike. "Just a few," he repeated for emphasis. He studied my eyes for some response, then looked up at the ceiling, apparently absorbed in a moment of obvious self-satisfaction.

I looked away and once more focused on the package of Demerol. It had to be someone with access to the narcotics cabinet, so that did narrow the number of possible suspects. But still, that would be a dozen or more nurses. The narcotics keys were handed off at the beginning and end of each shift, so there was an opportunity there for someone to put his or her hand on them. But the nurses were always careful with the keys, and they all understood how important this whole issue was. Their licenses and employment might depend on it.

"Let me tell you how this sort of thing works, Dr. Lesslie," Walter began, assuming the tone of one of his MBA professors. "It's very much like a case of embezzlement. The perpetrator has to fulfill three definite and specific criteria. First, they must have a need. This is almost always financial in nature. Secondly, they must have access—in this case, to the medication room and narcotics. And lastly, they must be able to rationalize their actions, overlooking the criminal nature of their activity and somehow justifying it. For some people, that's the easy part."

He paused, looking at me again, seeming satisfied with his fund of knowledge.

"Is it possible that the *perpetrator,* as you call them, might have a drug problem?" I asked him. "Maybe that's the case rather than a financial need. After all, these are small quantities of drugs we're missing, hardly a major deal on the streets of Rock Hill."

Out of the corner of my eye, I could see Virginia slowly nodding her head. But she remained silent.

"No, that's not the case here," Stevens said emphatically. "Whoever is stealing drugs from the ER is doing so because of money. They are selling whatever they can get their hands on and will continue doing so until we catch them. And that's what we're going to do. In fact, we—"

He stopped short, pursed his lips, and looked away from me.

"You're going to what?" I asked, curious where this last statement had been headed.

Walter slapped the armrests of his chair, stood up, and with an air of finality said, "Virginia, I'll be back with you in a couple of days. And we need to be sure this stays quiet. Not a word to any of your staff."

He glanced in my direction, and I thought there might be a hint of a warning in his eyes.

"Dr. Lesslie, good to see you as always." And with that, he turned and walked out of the office.

Virginia looked up at me and shook her head.

"Where do they find these people?" she asked in frustration. "You heard just a few minutes of it, but I've been in here for half an hour."

"What do you think he's talking about?" I asked her. "Who has he narrowed this down to? He seems so certain, but nobody comes to my mind. I can't imagine any of our people doing this. Yet…"

"Yet, it's happening," she finished my thought. "But he hasn't given me any specific names, just that he's got a good idea of who's doing this. He says he only needs a little more time and that he's 'gathering more information,' whatever that means. Anyway, it will be interesting to see what he comes up with. Maybe he knows something that we don't. And if he can help solve this, I will be glad for his assistance. We need to put a stop to it."

She was right about that. I stood up and walked to the door. Before opening it, I turned to her and said, "I might talk to Lori Davidson about this. She already knows about it, and she has a good read on people. Maybe she has an idea."

Virginia nodded her head and then pulled a pile of papers over in front of her. Without saying another word, she adjusted her glasses and went back to work.

At the nurses' station I was greeted with a "4-fer"—four patients for the price of one. The clipboard of room 5 held the charts of the four children I had seen heading into the ER. I guess they weren't visiting after all, but were now my patients. I looked down at the complaint written on the top chart, and then quickly at the other three.

Pinworms. Great.

I picked up the charts and was about to head to room 5, when the EMS radio came to life.

"Rock Hill ER, this is EMS 2."

Lori Davidson was standing beside Amy and she reached over and pushed the speakerphone button.

"EMS 2, this is the ER. Go ahead."

There was some painfully loud crackling, and Amy leaned over to adjust the volume.

"ER, we're on the way in with a traumatic arrest—twenty-two-year-old woman," the paramedic told us. It sounded like Denton Roberts, and he was out of breath or excited, or both.

I stopped where I was, put the charts back down on the counter, and glanced up at the clock—*9:15 a.m. It was early in the day for a traumatic arrest,* I thought. *Must be an auto accident.*

Lori was writing on a pad of paper beside the radio, shaking her head.

"Did you say 'twenty-two-year-old'?" she asked the paramedic.

"Yes," he responded. "Twenty-two, and pregnant. About thirty-eight to thirty-nine weeks."

Lori and I looked at each other. This last piece of information changed everything.

I leaned closer to the receiver and said, "Tell us what you have."

"Doc, this is Denton Roberts," he identified himself. "We're out on Cherry Road, two or three minutes away. Open head injury with no responses at all. I don't see any other obvious injuries. Blood pressure is 100 over 60 and her pulse is 110. Can't tell anything about the baby—too much noise to hear fetal heart tones."

He stopped and said something to someone in the background.

Then back to me he said, "She's intubated and we've got two lines in. Loading up right now. Anything else?"

I thought quickly. At this point, everything else needed to be done on our end.

"No, Denton. Just get here as fast as you can. Major trauma on arrival."

"Got that, Doc. Major trauma."

There was more crackling and then the radio went silent.

Lori was still looking at me, waiting for my directions.

"Do you want me to call anyone?" Amy Connors asked. "This sounds awful."

"Check upstairs in labor and delivery," I answered her. "See if one of the OBs is in the hospital. Maybe we'll get lucky."

Then turning to Lori: "Come on, we need to get things set up."

We only had a few minutes, but in that short time we managed to open up an airway tray and a general surgical tray, and had one of our techs bring the newborn warmer into the room.

"Plug that in over there," I directed her, pointing to a spot up near the head of the stretcher.

Lori had a concerned look on her face, and I thought I knew what she was thinking.

"No, I've never done an emergency C-section," I told her. "But I know what to do, and if there's no OB in the hospital, we'll get it done. Just don't go anywhere."

She nodded her head and turned around to the counter, making sure everything was ready. I was glad she was with me.

Thad Baxter stepped into trauma, and at the exact same instant I heard the automatic ambulance entrance doors open down the hallway.

"What have you got?" Thad asked, stepping over next to me. He was one of our OBs and must have just come out of a delivery. He was wearing a surgical cap and scrubs, and his right shoe cover had spattered blotches of blood on it. Boy, was I happy to see him.

"I came as fast as I could," he added, quickly glancing around the room.

I barely had enough time to tell him what little we knew, when the stretcher of EMS 2 was wheeled into the room. Denton Roberts was pushing the bed while at the same time bagging the young woman. His partner, Jamey, was walking beside the stretcher, trying to guide it with his body as he continued to do chest compressions.

"What happened?" I exclaimed, grabbing the stretcher and pulling it beside our bed. Only moments ago this woman had had a pulse and blood pressure. Once again, everything had changed.

Denton was flushed and obviously upset.

"We pulled into the parking lot and up to the door, and before we could get her out of the ambulance she went flatline," he explained hurriedly. "I mean…it just happened a couple of seconds ago."

We all worked together and got the young woman onto the trauma bed. Thad Baxter helped and then stepped back a little.

"Robert, we need to get this baby, and as fast as we can!"

"I think it's about a hundred," Lori said, taking her stethoscope from the woman's pregnant belly. "Strong and regular, though," she added.

The baby's heart rate was a little slow, but it was there, and that was something to be thankful for. I knew Thad was right—we needed to act quickly.

I began to examine her, making sure that the endotracheal tube was in the right position and that her breath sounds were normal. Then I checked her pupils. They were completely blown—as big as dimes, and unreactive to light. As I began to check the back of her head, Denton said, "There's a fair amount of her brains on Cherry Road."

Thad Baxter was stunned by this statement and looked back over his shoulder at the paramedic. He had moved over to the counter and was putting on some surgical gloves. One fell to the floor.

"Here," Lori said, handing him another pair.

The back of the woman's head was crushed, and there were large pieces of skull missing.

The obstetrician snapped his gloves in place, picked up a scalpel from the surgical tray, then turned to me and asked, "Does this woman have any chance?"

I looked down at her and then up into his eyes.

"No. None."

He stepped over to the side of the stretcher and completely exposed her abdomen. Denton's partner didn't miss a beat and kept doing his chest compressions.

"I'm going to hand you a baby in about two seconds, Robert," Thad told me. "So be ready."

Then without any hesitation he made an incision from just below her breastbone down to her pubis. There was very little bleeding, and the purplish mass of her uterus seemed to float up to us.

Another quick incision, and there was an arm and then a face.

Thad scooped the baby out of the uterus and handed a little boy to me. He was dusky, limp, and not making any effort to breathe.

"Hand me some surgical pads and some..."

Thad caught himself, and fell silent. This was no routine C-section, and he wouldn't be doing anything further for this baby's mother.

Jamey looked over at me and I nodded. He stopped doing his CPR, took a deep breath, and leaned heavily against the side of the stretcher.

"Let me know if I can help," Thad said to me, stepping close and looking over my shoulder.

"Lori, leave me some room with that umbilical cord in case we need to start a line," I said.

The nurse was getting ready to clamp the cord and then cut it. Sliding the clamp down another inch or so, she stopped and glanced up at me.

"That's fine," I told her, toweling off the boy, trying to stimulate him. We had already sucked out his airway and this hadn't elicited any reflex response. He was still dusky, and he had no muscle tone. But his heart rate was still around 100. There was still hope.

Suddenly his mouth opened and his eyes scrunched tightly closed. His hands came up toward us and he took a breath. We waited for what seemed an eternity, none of us breathing. And then he started. At first, his cries were feeble, almost tentative. But then he got mad and started hollering. His color quickly improved and he started kicking his legs.

"You go, boy!" Denton encouraged him from the foot of the stretcher. I looked up at Lori and saw tears running down her face.

Thad put his hand on my shoulder and said, "Well, will you look at that."

While we celebrated this miracle, relieved and emotionally exhausted, his mother lay only a few feet away, dead.

Denton told us what had happened out on Cherry Road. And it was only then that we learned the woman's name was Nicki Tyler. She had been at the grocery store with a friend, when her water broke.

Nicki had a four-year-old daughter, and she knew what to do.

"Let me drive you to the hospital," her friend had volunteered.

But Nicki insisted she would be fine, and if her friend wanted to follow her, that would be great.

At the scene of the accident, Nicki's friend had told Denton what she had witnessed. She had been directly behind Nicki the whole time and had seen everything.

"It was like slow motion," she had said. "I knew what was going to happen, but I couldn't do anything to stop it."

She told Denton that Nicki was a very careful driver and always wore her seatbelt.

"Her belly must have been hurting after her water broke," she had surmised. "Maybe she was having contractions, 'cause I saw her take off her belt when we stopped at one of the red lights. Then we drove on down Cherry Road and when we came to the next intersection, the light was red and I started slowing down. But Nicki didn't. It was as if she didn't see it or was looking somewhere else, but she just went straight through it. That's when the pickup truck T-boned her from the passenger side and her door busted open and she went flying through the air. It was awful, just like I said, slow motion...and I couldn't do anything to help her. She landed on the back of her head and bounced a couple of times, then just lay there in the middle of the road. I...I didn't know what to do."

It made sense now. This explained the head injury and the lack of any other obvious trauma. Thankfully she wouldn't have known anything once she hit the pavement.

I was standing by the stretcher, looking down at Nicki's face. Lori had put a fresh pillow under her head and covered her body with a clean sheet. She looked peaceful, almost as if she were sleeping.

Now Lori was swaddling the baby in a warming blanket over his loud and persistent objections. He was going to be fine and in a few minutes would be taken up to pediatrics.

"Her husband should be out front any time now," Lori said quietly, not looking up at me.

I knew I had to do this, but I had never been in this situation before. How was I going to tell him about his wife?

I stepped over to the door, opened it, and looked back once more at Nicki Tyler and her son. This time Lori looked up at me and smiled. It was a mixture of sadness and encouragement, and it was what I needed. I stepped out into the hallway, closed the trauma room door behind me, and immediately froze.

There in front of the nurses' station was a young man, leaning over the counter a little and talking to Amy Connors. Standing by his right side was a little girl. One of her hands clutched her father's pants leg, while the thumb of her other was in her mouth.

With her large, brown, unblinking eyes, she was looking straight at me.

9

Hoodooed

6:58 a.m. Liz Kennick was standing at the nurses' station writing on a chart and shaking her head. She was upset about something.

Angie Weathers was sitting at the desk beside Amy as I walked up. She caught my eye and shook her head mysteriously. *What was going on?*

"Okay, time for you to go home," I said to Liz, trying to be cheerful. "Anything to turn over?"

She signed her name to the bottom of the chart and then threw her pen down on the counter.

"This guy—" she said, spitting out the words and jabbing the paper in front of her with her index finger. "This guy did a number on me!"

The clipboard was for room 2, and I looked across the nurses' station to that cubicle. The curtain was drawn open and the room was empty.

Amy looked up at me, then rolled her eyes just a bit. She was trying hard not to smile.

"He did what?" I asked her, leaning closer to the counter and reading the record in front of her. The patient's name was James Wiley III, and he was twenty-eight years old. "Chest pain, fever, and cancer," was the listed complaint.

"He worked me over, Robert," Liz answered angrily. "And I don't like it."

This sounded interesting, and I couldn't resist. "Tell me about it," I encouraged her.

This time Amy put her hand to her mouth and swiveled around in her chair with her back to us.

Liz apparently didn't notice this, and she began to tell me the story of James Wiley III.

"This guy came in a couple of hours ago, maybe four or four-thirty. We were still pretty busy and Angie brought him back from triage and put him in room 2. 'Nothing urgent,' she told me, so I kept working with my other patients."

I glanced down at Angie. She raised her eyebrows and nodded her head in agreement.

"I got to him about twenty minutes later," Liz continued. "When I went in the room, he was sort of clutching his chest and rocking back and forth on the stretcher. It seemed like he was in a lot of pain. He got down and started pacing the floor and really had me worried. Then he proceeded to tell me about his medical history. A few years earlier, he had been diagnosed with some kind of lymphoma. He showed me a scar on his chest where he said the doctors at Johns Hopkins had done a biopsy to determine the extent of his disease."

She paused for a moment and her eyes narrowed. "I should have suspected something then!" she exclaimed. "I didn't look closely at the scar—he just raised his shirt for a split second and pointed to it and then pulled his shirt back down. But now that I think about it, that wasn't a very likely location for a biopsy. I should have known.

"Anyway, he told me he had been in remission for a year or two and had done well up until three months ago. The lymphoma had come back and was in his chest, pressing on blood vessels and nerves and causing a lot of pain. That's when he first asked me for some oxyco-done."

"That should have been the tip-off," Amy muttered.

Liz shot her an icy glare and then looked back over at me.

"This guy had a folder full of medical records," she continued to explain. "And when I took a look at some of them, they seemed to support his story. All he needed was just enough pain medicine to make it back home to Tennessee, to his oncologist. It was just going to be a few days and…well…"

"Let me guess," I interjected. "He's allergic to every drug known to man except oxycodone. Am I right?"

For a split second Liz seemed to want to stiffen her neck, but instead she looked up sheepishly. "Yes, that's right. And I should have known better. But it was five in the morning, and I was tired, and he seemed legit, and—"

"And let me guess again," I interrupted once more. "There was no name on the medical records. Not his, not anyone's."

She jerked her head up at this apparently new and shocking revelation. "I don't know, Robert! I didn't even look. But come to think of it, I didn't notice anybody's name on those records. Just his on the outside of that folder. And he could have—"

"Of course he did," Amy jumped in. "He wrote his own name on it, if it was really his name."

"But he would've had to have some kind of ID to present at the drugstore, wouldn't he?" Angie asked. "I mean, the pharmacist wouldn't have filled the prescription without a picture ID of some sort, right?"

"You wrote him a prescription?" I asked Liz, a little surprised. She was fresh out of her residency, but she seemed to be way too savvy to have fallen for this kind of ruse.

There was that sheepish look again.

"Just for a few," she answered quietly.

"A few?" Amy exclaimed. "How about 40? And then he tried to change the 4 to an 8!"

"What?" I asked, only a little surprised by his brazenness. I had once had a drug-seeker change my prescription for pain meds from 12 to 120. Fortunately the pharmacist had caught that one, just like someone must have caught this guy.

"Yeah, pretty crazy, right?" Amy said, chuckling and shaking her head. "The pharmacist out near the interstate called and asked us about that. And then he proceeded to tell us he did some checkin' online and found that Mr. James Wiley III has been quite busy. This was his sixth prescription in the past 24 hours, all for oxycodone and all from different ERs." She folded her arms across her chest, smiled, and with feigned condescension looked over at our at newest ER doctor.

"Don't feel bad," Angie began. "He must have—"

"Well I *do* feel bad!" Liz interrupted. "I should have been paying more attention. I should have known from the very beginning that something was up."

She was getting angry again, and her face was starting to flush. I needed to rescue her.

"Liz, it happens to all of us," I tried to calm her. "Some of these folks are pretty clever, and they know we're busy and trying to take care of a lot of people as quickly as we can. And just so you know, his coming in at four in the morning was not just by chance. It was carefully calculated on his part. He was hoping you would be tired and would just want to get him taken care of as quickly as you could."

"And he was right," she admitted. "But still, I should have known better."

Her eyes once again focused on Wiley's chart, and she didn't say anything. Then suddenly she must have thought of something and she looked up at me. "What about you, Robert? If it happens to everybody, then when was the last time someone pulled one over on you?"

"Me?" I responded in mock surprise.

"Yeah, you, Dr. Lesslie," Amy interjected. Then she turned to Liz and said, "But hoodooed would be more like it."

"What exactly do you mean by 'hoodooed'?" I inquired, glaring at the secretary.

"You know what I mean," Amy replied with an eyebrow raised. "Tell them about Charlene Saunders and Adelle."

She had me, and I quietly surrendered. "Oh...Charlene."

It had been the middle of winter and an ice storm had just blown through York County. At two in the morning, most people were home in their beds and were not venturing out onto the treacherous roads. For those of us in the ER, the quiet was welcome. We had only seen a handful of people since seven in the evening, and it looked like we might be done for the night.

Then the triage door opened and Jeff Ryan led a young woman into the department. She was carrying a four- or five-year-old girl in her arms, and Jeff led them to room 5.

"Well, so much for it being too icy to be getting out," said Susan, our unit secretary. She sat up in her chair and reopened the ER logbook, preparing to make a new entry. "It did look like that child was pretty sick, though," she added.

Jeff walked back over to where we sat and dropped down into his chair. Then he handed me the chart of room 5 and said, "I don't think we've ever seen this one. Mother says they're new to town and don't have a doctor yet. The child has some kind of cerebral palsy and has run out of her medication."

I held the chart in my hands and scanned the front page. The girl's name was Adelle Saunders and she was five years old. Jeff had written down the chief complaint—"Out of medicine—chloral hydrate. Now agitated."

"Agitated?" I asked him. "She looked like she was asleep when you walked by the counter," I observed.

"Hard to say," Jeff answered slowly. "She doesn't walk, and when her mother put her down on the stretcher, she sat there leaning against the rail and then started banging her head against the wall. Not hard or anything, just kinda…well, I guess she was banging it. Her mother says she does it all the time when she's out of her medicine."

Chloral hydrate. Now *that* was an old drug. During my training, some of the pediatricians on staff would use it to sedate kids before procedures that required them to be calm and still. It was effective, but sometimes difficult to dose correctly. And it had the potential to be abused.

"I wonder where she's been getting the chloral hydrate," I mused.

"Isn't that the old 'knockout drops'?" Jeff asked. "Like you used to see in the movies?"

"Yeah, you're right," I responded, reminded of this romanticized use of the drug. "It's the old 'Mickey Finn.'"

"Mickey Finn?" Susan asked, curious. She was too young to know anything about this. "What in the world is a 'Mickey Finn'?"

I thought for a moment but couldn't remember where this name had come from. Then realizing I probably had never known, I stood up and looked down at her.

"Jeff will explain that one," I told her. "I've got to go see the child in 5."

The mother of Adelle Saunders looked up as I entered the room.

"Ms. Saunders," I greeted the young woman. "I'm Dr. Lesslie. And this is your daughter?"

"Yes," she answered, smiling. "This is Adelle, and I'm Charlene Saunders."

I walked over to the stool at the head of the stretcher and sat down.

"Tell me what brings you to the ER this morning," I began.

Charlene Saunders proceeded to share with me her daughter's complicated medical history and her problems with cerebral palsy.

"She has the mental age of a one-year-old," she patiently explained. "About a year ago, she became very difficult to manage. That's when she started this head-banging of hers."

I had noticed this persistent, rhythmic movement of Adelle's but hadn't said anything about it yet. She was slowly rocking back and forth and tapping her head against the wall beside the stretcher. Not hard, and I don't think it was hurting her. But I thought it a little peculiar that it didn't seem to be bothering her mother very much. Maybe she was used to it. After a few minutes though, it had started to get to me.

"Why don't you hold her in your lap," I suggested, hoping her mother would be able to control the compulsive behavior.

"No, she's fine," Charlene responded, smiling at me again. "Anyway, the only thing the doctors in Raleigh found that would help her was chloral hydrate. It was like a miracle! When she takes it, she's just as calm and sweet as can be. And she never does any of this," she added, tilting her head toward Adelle.

"So she's been taking it for a year?" I asked. That was a little odd, and you would have to worry about the potential for dependence, if not addiction.

"That's about right," she answered, nodding her head. "And if we ever run out, then this starts again. That's what happened today. We haven't been able to find a doctor in Rock Hill yet, and she took her last dose about twelve hours ago. That's why we're here now, to get enough to last her until we can get in to see a pediatrician. Probably a week or so."

She sat there, and waited for my response.

"Well, let's take a look at her," I said, standing up and moving beside the bed.

She didn't have any fever and I couldn't find evidence of any significant trauma. The right side of her head was a little red from where she had been hitting the wall, but nothing else.

She was a pretty girl, with curly blonde hair and light blue eyes. The cerebral palsy had left her with contorted limbs, with her left arm drawn up to her chest and her legs permanently flexed at the knees. She was able to use her right arm to move herself around and shift positions.

"Can she speak?" I asked Charlene, looking down at the child and smiling.

"She's never said a word," her mother answered flatly. "The doctors say she never will."

We talked a little more, and I gave her some advice about who I thought would be the best pediatricians for her daughter. When they left the department, I gave her a prescription for a week's worth of chloral hydrate. No refills.

"Thank you, Dr. Lesslie," Charlene said as they passed the nurses' station and went back out to the waiting room.

The rest of the night passed uneventfully, and no one else seemed willing to brave the dangerous roads. We soon forgot about Charlene and Adelle Saunders.

About two weeks later, we knew we might have a problem. One of my partners, Ted Nivens, had seen Charlene and Adelle during the middle of the night. He thought it a little unusual, and he told me about it when I relieved him at 7 a.m. Jeff had not been working, nor had Susan. If they had been, they might have been able to tip Ted off.

The visit had been a carbon copy of the first. Charlene was asking for enough chloral hydrate until she could see a pediatrician. "Just enough to get Adelle by," she had persisted. Ted had the old record in front of him and could read what I had done.

"I was reluctant to do this again," he told me. "But she was begging me, and that poor child just kept banging her head on the wall. Finally I gave in and wrote her enough for three days only. I told her that was all we could do, and that she needed to have her medication refilled by Adelle's doctor. What else could I do?"

There wasn't much else he could have done. It's one thing to refuse an adult who is demanding narcotics, but it's something entirely different when a child is involved. Especially a child who is so dependent on her mother.

"You did the right thing," I told him. "Hopefully she'll find her daughter a pediatrician before she runs out of medicine again."

She didn't. And a few days later they were back in the ER. This time, they saw another doctor, and again they got more medication. Lori Davidson showed me the record the next morning and asked what I thought we should do.

"Let's give Charlene Saunders a call," I told her, searching the ER record for a phone number.

I dialed the number and waited.

"The number you have dialed is not in service. Please—"

I pressed the receiver button down and tried again.

"The number you have—"

Angrily, I hung up the phone.

"You're not surprised, are you?" Amy Connors asked, having heard the story and watched my futile efforts.

"I guess I shouldn't be," I sulked. "What do we do now?"

"I suppose we'll have to wait until she comes back in," Lori said calmly. "Then we'll address this with her and make sure she understands. If she comes in during the day, we can arrange for a pediatrician to see her right then."

That sounded perfectly reasonable, but thus far, Charlene seemed to know the best time to come to the ER for something like this, and it wasn't during regular office hours.

"We'll see," I said doubtfully.

We didn't hear from the Saunderses for a while. Several weeks went by, and I had almost forgotten about them. Then it started again. Charlene would bring Adelle to the ER during the middle of the night and ask yet again for chloral hydrate. She would beg the ER doctor on duty while her daughter banged her head against the wall of the exam room. Ted tried once or twice to be firm with her, but ultimately relented. She seemed to be intentionally avoiding *me* though, and while I heard about their visits, they never showed up while I was working. Not until the week before Easter.

It was the middle of the night again, and into the ER walked Charlene, once more carrying Adelle. It was the same story, but with a little different twist this time. Charlene had managed to find a pediatrician for her daughter, but he was vacationing out of the country and couldn't be reached. It was 3 a.m., and how were we going to confirm or refute that? She needed enough chloral hydrate for two weeks and we were her only hope of getting it. No one else in town would write it for her.

"Look at her!" Charlene had pleaded, pointing to her daughter. "It's getting worse, and I can't control her. This goes on all night."

Adelle *did* seem to be more agitated this time, and there were bruises on the side of her head, not just some faint redness. Against my better judgment, I gave her a week's worth of the medicine and said, "This is it, Charlene. No more. Do you understand?"

"I understand, Dr. Lesslie," she said, taking the prescription and stuffing it in her purse. "And thank you. This will be the last time I ever ask you to do this. Ever."

She turned and walked out of the department. Jeff Ryan was standing on the other side of the counter, looking at me and shaking his head.

But Charlene kept her word. She never asked me again for chloral hydrate. It would be Ted Nivens, and it was two days later. This time, the gig was up.

"I couldn't believe it," Ted had told me. "She came in during the afternoon, right in the middle of the day when we were really busy. They were in room 4, and when I walked in I almost fell over. There was this sickeningly sweet odor in the room, and Charlene had this reddish liquid on her chin and it was spilled all over her blouse. Her eyes were glazed and her speech was slurred. And there was Adelle on the stretcher like she always is. Then the woman had the audacity to ask for more chloral hydrate for her daughter! I just looked at her and knew I was about to blow. She started demanding that I write her a prescription and stood up and shook her finger in my face. She almost fell over on the floor. It was all I could do to get her back on the stretcher so she wouldn't hurt herself."

Now it all made sense. This woman had been taking Adelle's medicine all along, if in fact it had ever been given to her daughter in the first place.

"What did you do with her?" I asked Ted.

"Well, we put her in observation for a couple of hours," he explained. "And one of our techs watched Adelle. Then when Charlene could walk straight, we called a cab. I had a word of prayer with her and told her that if she ever came in again asking for chloral hydrate, we would call the police, or something worse. She seemed to understand, though. And before she left, we gave her some information about where she could get some help for her addiction. I was going to call DSS, but she was gone before I could. But I don't think we'll be seeing her again."

"We need to call DSS anyway," I suggested. "Adelle doesn't need to spend the rest of her life like this."

Less than a week later, we learned that she wouldn't. Adelle was dead. We didn't find out about it until the afternoon Charlene was brought to the ER by EMS. She had called 9-1-1, hysterical and totally out of control. A day or so earlier, her daughter had had a seizure and apparently aspirated. Charlene blamed herself and was inconsolable.

"When we got to her apartment building," Denton Roberts told us, "she was walking up and down the sidewalk, waving her arms in the air and screaming. The neighbors couldn't get her calmed down, and we were barely able to get her to lie down on the stretcher."

Ted Nivens had been on duty when she came in. It took him a while to get her to the point where he could talk with her. She had no family in the area and no friends, but she didn't want to be admitted to the hospital.

"I'll be okay," she had tried to convince him. "It will take a while, without Adelle, but…"

And then she broke down all over again. Ted was worried she might try to hurt herself. After all, she hadn't proven herself to be the most dependable and upright of people. But in the end, she calmed down and he was able to send her home. He gave her something to help her rest, but it wouldn't be chloral hydrate this time.

A week later, I was finishing up a night shift when Ted Nivens walked through the ambulance entrance doors.

I told him about the patient in room 5 who was over in radiology getting a chest X-ray for a possible collapsed lung. And I told him that Charlene Saunders had come in during the middle of the night.

"She told me she was doing okay, but that every once in a while, she just lost it," I told him. "I refilled the Valium you gave her and told her she needed to follow up with somebody at the mental-health clinic."

I thought Ted was going to explode. His face turned red and steam started pouring out of his ears.

"You gave her more Valium?" he exclaimed. "Why that…"

He sputtered for a minute, searching for the right words. Then he took a deep breath and said, "I've been off for a couple of days and haven't had a chance to talk with you. I guess I should have called, but I've been busy."

"Call me about what?" I asked, curious about his reaction and now this last statement.

"Well, Robert, let me just tell you about our Charlene Saunders," he began. "About a week ago, I was out at Wal-Mart picking up a couple of things and just looking around. I think I was in the sporting goods department when I turned a corner and started down an aisle. I wasn't paying much attention and almost ran into the back of a woman who had stopped in front of some fishing tackle. I said, 'Excuse me,' and when she turned around, doggone if it wasn't Charlene. Her eyes got real big and she looked like she had seen a ghost or something. She started backing away, pulling her cart, and that's when I looked down."

He stopped talking and his face got red again.

"What happened?" I asked him, confused. "Why did she—"

"Robert," he interrupted me. "I looked down in that cart, and there sat Adelle, big as life. She was smiling and looking around, and... and..."

My mouth dropped open and I was speechless.

"I just stood there and stared at the two of them," he told me, calmer now. "I couldn't say anything, and Charlene just kept backing down that aisle, then turned a corner and disappeared. She never said a word."

Hoodooed—all the way around.

10

Lost

It was several days after our meeting with Walter Stevens before I had a chance to talk with Lori Davidson. It was a little after seven in the morning, and I was washing my hands in the medicine room when she walked in.

"Lori, have you got a second?" I asked her, drying my hands on some paper towels.

"Sure. Just getting some Rocephin for the child in room 2," she answered. She put down the chart in her hand, took a key chain out of her pocket, and unlocked one of the drug cabinets. We kept our injectable medicines, such as antibiotics and nausea drugs, locked up in a floor-to-ceiling cabinet. Beside that cabinet was the narcotic storage container. It was double-locked, requiring two different keys to open.

"You're the one who found the missing Vistaril," I began. "And I'm sure you know about the unaccounted-for narcotics."

She stopped and looked at me, her key still in the cabinet lock.

"Yes, I do," she answered, her voice serious and subdued. There was a frown on her face, something unusual for Lori.

"Does any of this make sense to you?" I asked her. "I mean, I don't know who in this department would be messing with the narcotics. It would have to be someone with access to the keys, and even then… they'd have to be pretty brazen to be getting stuff out of the cabinet in plain sight, don't you think?"

She sighed and shook her head. "I've been thinking a lot about this,

Dr. Lesslie. And I've started watching different people, and wondering…I just can't imagine any of our staff doing this."

"You know about the Demerol vials," I continued. "I've never seen anything like that. Walter Stevens showed me that box the other day, and I couldn't believe it."

"Walter Stevens," Lori muttered, in a tone as close to disgust as I had ever heard from her. "He's on some kind of a crusade, it seems. And if I hear about his *bus* one more time, I think I'll explode."

"His 'bus'?" I asked her, confused. "What are you talking about?"

"I've been in a few meetings with him, and he always talks about '*the bus.*' He compares the hospital to a big bus, and he talks about making sure the right people are on the bus and in the right seats. And if they don't need to be on the bus, or shouldn't be on it—well, he's going to make sure they get off. I'm sure he just wants the hospital to be the best it can be, but sometimes he seems a little obsessive."

It sounded like some kind of management style he had learned in business school, but I had never heard him mention it.

"He's determined to solve this problem and have someone prosecuted," Lori added. "I hope it's not all about making himself look good, because somebody out there is in trouble and needs our help."

I thought about this for a moment, realizing Lori's perspective had been lost on me. Like Stevens, I wanted this figured out, and quickly. And I hadn't considered this point of view, that whoever was doing this might have a real problem and need our assistance. Lori was right, but the first thing was to find out who this person was—maybe *persons*. Whoa—that was something else I hadn't considered.

"And this idea of Mr. Stevens that someone is *selling* these drugs," she continued, shaking her head. "That's crazy. I think someone is stealing the stuff and using it themselves, as bad as that sounds."

"I think you're right," I said. "I tried to tell Stevens that the small amount of missing drugs wouldn't add up to very much on the street, certainly not enough to be worth the risk of losing your job. He just wouldn't listen. But you know, before that meeting with Virginia and him, I was hoping this was all some mistake, some counting or documentation error. And then there was that box of Demerol. That's no counting error."

I tossed the paper towels in the trash can and was about to say something else, when Lori glanced at the door and quietly said, "I need to show you something."

She took the key out of the antibiotic cabinet, sorted through the chain for another pair of keys, and opened the narcotics cabinet. There were several boxes of medication, just like the Demerol container, and she reached for one in the back of one of the shelves.

"I found this when I first came in," she said, handing it to me. "Darren Adler worked last night, and he did the drug count with me. I didn't say anything to him, because I don't know who all knows about this. I was going to bring Ms. Granger in here just as soon as I took care of the child in room 2."

I knew where to look this time, and I turned the box upside down. The plastic wrapper was still in place, but once again, there were several small holes in the bottom. I counted five, evenly spaced, just like before.

Shaking my head, I handed the Demerol back to Lori.

"I wonder if this could be dusted for prints," I thought aloud.

"I was thinking the same thing," she agreed. "But then I thought about how many people have handled this. There's whoever delivered it to the hospital, and the people in the pharmacy—and every time we count the narcotics somebody picks it up. And now there's you," she added, smiling.

"Hmm…" I murmured, looking down at my hands. "Well, I guess that's not going to help. But I agree, you need to let Virginia know. This is worse than I thought. Maybe the three of us can talk about it later."

"What about Walter Stevens?" she asked, her frown returning. "Do you think he needs to know about this?"

"*I* wouldn't tell him, Lori," I said. "He's got enough information to run with, it seems. But I'd let Virginia make that call."

"You're right," she agreed, putting the Demerol back in the cabinet and double-locking the doors.

"Do you have any idea who might be doing this?" I pursued. "Any unusual behavior or strange activity? 'Cause I haven't."

"I haven't either," she spoke quietly, slowly shaking her head and studying the floor. Then she looked up at me and said, "But I'm paying more attention now. And if someone is using this stuff, it's only a matter of time before they slip up, or do something stupid, or worse."

Again she was right, And I was worried about the "or worse" part.

"I will be too," I told her, stepping toward the doorway. "And if you see something, or find more punctured boxes of Demerol, let me know."

I left her in the medicine room with the chart of room 2 and walked over to the nurses' station, deep in thought and a little confused—and very troubled.

8:30 a.m. I didn't know if Lori had had a chance to talk with Virginia, but I hadn't. A few minutes after I walked out of the medicine room the floodgates had opened. There was a minor school bus accident out on highway 21, and EMS had brought in a dozen or so kids to be examined. Fortunately no one was really injured, but they all needed to be checked over.

And then we had a construction worker who fell off some scaffolding at his work site. He ended up being diagnosed with fractures of both heels. That wasn't a life threatening injury, but it was a life-changing one. He would never walk the same and would probably always have pain in those feet. It happens so fast.

"Here, Amy," I said, sliding the chart of this patient across the counter. "We need to get in touch with ortho and make sure they see him as soon as possible."

"Sure," she answered, picking up the chart and putting it on top of the pile beside her. "Just as soon as I get some of these schoolkids straightened out."

The ambulance doors burst open and a man who looked about thirty ran into the department.

"Help me!" he yelled. "Somebody help me!"

He was carrying a little girl in his arms, and as he looked around the ER for assistance, her arms and legs flopped lifelessly. She didn't appear to be breathing.

He was panicking, twisting from side to side, taking a step in one direction and then another. I hurried over to him and took the child from his arms.

"Follow me," I directed him, heading to the cardiac room. Jeff Ryan was a couple of steps ahead of me and I called to him, "We need an airway tray!" He didn't need to respond, but I saw his head nod as he disappeared into the room.

"Amy, call radiology," I ordered over my shoulder. "And get the lab down here. And respiratory therapy," I added.

I took a look down at the little girl. She couldn't have been older than three, and her color was terrible. She was a dark blue and hung like a wet towel in my arms. It was then I noticed the mucus coming out of her nose and a foamy substance coming from her mouth. And I was right—she wasn't breathing.

"We'll need suction," I told Jeff as I carefully placed her on our stretcher.

"Right here," he said, handing me the suction catheter, then turning to flip its switch on the wall behind him.

I cleared as much of the mucus from her nose and mouth as I could, and within another thirty seconds we had her airway secured with an endotracheal tube.

One of our respiratory therapists had just walked into the room and over to where I stood.

"Here, let me do that," he said, taking the ambu bag and beginning to rhythmically inflate the girl's chest.

"Thanks," I told him, leaning down and placing my stethoscope on her chest, first on one side and then the other.

"That's good," I said. "She sounds wet, but we're getting good breath sounds on both sides."

Jeff had attached cardiac electrodes to her chest and now flipped on the monitor. At first there was just some chaotic activity, nothing that looked like any purposeful electrical impulses. But after a few seconds, we began to see some narrow, regular complexes—about thirty or forty a minute. That was slow and wouldn't sustain her for very long. I hoped that providing oxygen to her lungs would fix that, and that her heart rate would quickly come up to where it should be—some place over 100.

The man who had brought the little girl had been standing quietly in a corner of the room. I assumed he was her father, and I turned to him and asked, "Is this your daughter?"

"Yes, it is," he answered, barely audible. "Trish. Her name is Trish." He was wringing his hands and I noticed how flushed he was. He was sweating, and his soiled T-shirt was plastered to his chest. I looked down and saw his blue jeans and grass-stained sneakers. He must have been working outside earlier this morning, maybe mowing grass.

"Can you tell us what happened?" I asked him.

Behind me, the radiology tech wheeled her portable machine into the room and beside the stretcher. She would be getting a chest X-ray to check on tube placement and for anything that might be going on in this little girl's chest. The lab tech was drawing blood from her right elbow and Jeff was starting an IV in her left arm. It was controlled chaos, and there was a lot of noise. I stepped closer to the man so I could hear him.

He continued to wring his hands, and his eyes darted from place to place around the room, then focused back on his daughter.

He didn't look up at me when I repeated, "Can you tell us what happened?"

"I was out in the yard, working…" he stammered. "I was just…I never thought it would…"

I leaned closer, trying to make out what he was saying.

"You were what?" I tried again.

"Dr. Lesslie," Jeff called out to me. "Heart rate's less than 30 and I don't feel much of a pulse."

I turned from the man and stepped back to the stretcher and the little girl. Her color might have been a little better, but she still wasn't responding or making any effort to breathe. I looked over at the monitor. Jeff was right. Her heart rate was still dangerously slow. But why? With most kids, when you took care of their breathing, their heart rate would fix itself and improve. What was going on here?

"Look at her pupils," Jeff said to me. He had raised both of her eyelids and was shining a flashlight into one and then the other. They were pinpoint and didn't react to light. When the lids wouldn't shut on their own, Jeff gently closed them.

"What do you make of that?" he asked me, searching my face for an answer. I wasn't sure. Lack of oxygen usually makes a person's pupils dilate, not constrict.

I was about to answer him when the X-ray tech came back into the room with the developed film and said, "Dr. Lesslie, you'll want to look at this."

She walked over to the view box, snapped the X-ray in place, then switched on the light.

As I quickly stepped across the room, I could tell from a distance that the endotracheal tube was in good position and where it should be. But as I got closer, I could see something was wrong—very wrong.

Her lungs were almost whited-out—full of fluid. It was the kind of chest X-ray you would expect to see in an elderly patient with end-stage heart failure. But her heart size was normal. What would—

I spun around and called out to Jeff, "Give her an amp of atropine! And then get ready for some more. She's going to need a lot of it."

Turning in the direction of the girl's father, I walked over and got right in his face. "What were you trying to tell me?" I asked him, more forcefully now. I needed answers, and I needed them fast. "What were you doing out in your yard? And what was Trish doing?"

His eyes were glassy now, vacant. And he kept wringing his hands and sweating.

"We've got those army worms," he said in a hoarse whisper. "They've killed most of the lawns in our neighborhood, and I was just trying to save ours. I didn't think it would…" his voice trailed off and he just stared over at Trish.

"You didn't think what?" I demanded, trying to get his attention. "Were you using some kind of insecticide? Some kind of poison?"

"Sevin," he answered, almost mouthing the word. "The man at the hardware store told me to use Sevin dust. I was spreading it in the front yard and I…I wasn't paying attention. There was a breeze blowing in my face, and no dust was getting on me. I just kept spreading it…and… and I didn't know Trish had come out of the house and was walking behind me. I didn't know…"

He stopped wringing his hands and tightly clutched both sides of his face. Then he started crying and rocking from side to side.

"She was lying on the grass," he struggled between pain-filled gasps. "And there was dust all over her face and mouth and nose. And she was barely breathing. I grabbed her and jumped in the car and came straight here."

He suddenly stopped, stood up straight, and started looking around the room.

"Where's my wife?" he called out. "Where's Fay?"

"Heart rate's still around 40," Jeff called out to me. "More atropine?"

I glanced at the monitor and then back to the man in front of me.

"Have a seat here," I gently instructed him, guiding him to another stool in the far corner of the room. Then motioning to one of our techs, I said, "Stay here with him and try to keep him calm."

Satisfied that he was being taken care of, I stepped back over to the side of the stretcher.

"Jeff, we need to get Amy to call the pharmacy for some 2-PAM. They'll know what it is, and we'll figure out a dose when we get it."

Atropine was the first drug to be used for this poisoning, but 2-PAM was a more specific antidote. She might need a lot of it if she was going to make it out of the ER.

For the next hour and a half, we worked feverishly to save Trish. We were battling a potent enemy, and it looked like we were losing. Sevin belongs to a group of chemicals that are very effective in killing harmful insects. But in heavy doses they are also harmful to humans, especially children. They cause nausea and vomiting, muscle spasms, increased secretions, and a slow heart rate. Seizures and death can occur, especially in the very young, like Trish. Fortunately, the treatment is centered around the use of a couple of readily available compounds.

After two or three adult-sized doses of atropine, her heart rate got as high as 96 and she had a detectable blood pressure. We used the 2-PAM and things began to stabilize a little. She even began to make some purposeful movements with her arms and hands.

Her father (we found out his name was John Sessions) continued to sit on his stool in the corner of the room, staring blankly at his daughter. He didn't get up when his wife, Fay, came into cardiac.

She immediately ran over to the stretcher and tried to hug her daughter, screaming her name and resisting Jeff as he gently kept her from disrupting our efforts. She finally calmed down when she was able to stand by the head of the bed and stroke Trish's hair.

"I'm here, baby," she whispered over and over.

Occasionally she would turn around and look at her husband, searching for answers and some support—*anything* from him. There was never a response. He just sat there, staring at the stretcher, his hands tightly clasping his knees.

By eleven o'clock we had done all we could in the ER, and Trish was on her way up to the pediatric ICU. She was stable, as far as her heart rate and blood pressure were concerned, and she was starting to make some efforts at breathing. But she continued to be mostly unresponsive, showing only the occasional movement of her hands. She didn't respond to pain and her pupils still didn't react to light, though they were larger now. We would just have to wait and see. It was a matter of time, and it was out of our hands.

John and Fay Sessions followed their daughter out of cardiac and down the hallway, leaving Jeff and me alone in the room.

He was trying to clean up the mess created by more than two hours of frantic activity, while I stood at the counter and tried to document what had just happened.

"I'm worried about the girl's father," Jeff quietly observed while reeling in dozens of feet of cardiac monitor paper strewn haphazardly on the floor. "He's still in a daze. I'm not sure he knows what's going on."

"He knows," I told him. "He just doesn't know how to handle it. That was his daughter lying there, and in his mind, he caused this. Of course it was an accident, but I don't think he sees it that way."

"That's what I mean," he agreed, standing up straight and looking over at me. "I'm worried about how he's gonna deal with it. I remember when I was teaching my daughter to ride a bike and she fell and broke her wrist. It was a simple greenstick fracture and did fine, but it killed me. I beat myself up about that for a long time. Still bothers me when I think about it. But this…this is a whole different thing. And I don't know how I would…" his voice trailed off and he was silent.

I nodded my head in understanding. "Let's just hope she recovers," I sighed, turning once again to my charting.

The next morning, Ted Nivens was telling me about the elderly woman he was leaving me in ortho. She had tripped and fallen while getting up to go to the bathroom and had broken her right hip. We were waiting on her labs and for the orthopedist to come down and admit her.

"That's all I've got for you," he told me, and then headed toward the ambulance doors. He only took a few steps before he stopped and turned around.

"Oh, and you might be hearing something from the folks upstairs," he added, moving closer and lowering his voice.

"The folks upstairs?" I asked.

"Yeah, the nurses in the CCU," he began to explain. "Jane Plexico, specifically. The new charge nurse."

"Why? What happened?" I was curious now.

"Darren was the nurse working with me last night, and we had two patients that needed to be admitted to the CCU. We were just waiting on beds, and as usual, it was taking a long time. But for some reason, it was really long last night, and Darren went upstairs to see what was going on. Apparently he found the staff sitting in their lounge, talking, and not getting either of the rooms ready. It had been more than four hours, and he exploded."

Knowing Darren Adler, I could easily imagine that happening, and I probably wouldn't have blamed him.

"What happened after that?" I asked Ted.

"Well, both of our patients were upstairs in the unit in less than twenty minutes," he told me, chuckling. "But there will probably be some fallout. Just wanted to give you the heads-up."

He turned around, and this time he made it through the doors.

They had just closed behind him when—"Code Blue! Pediatric ICU! Code Blue! Pediatric ICU!"

It was the hospital intercom, and there was an arrest upstairs in the unit. I looked down at Amy Connors and said, "Here—hold this!"

I dropped my briefcase on the countertop and hurried down the hallway toward the staff elevators in the back of the building. The pediatric ICU was on the fourth floor, and when I got to the elevator, one of the respiratory therapy techs was standing there holding the door open for me.

"Thought I heard somebody running this way," he said. "Peds ICU?"

"Yeah," I responded. "Thanks."

The doors closed and I stood there, impatiently watching the panel of floor buttons as they lit up one by one.

"Must be that insecticide kid, the one poisoned by her father," the tech said from behind me. I didn't turn around, knowing he was probably right and not wanting to respond.

"Not many other children in the unit right now, and they're all doing okay," he added.

The elevator doors opened and we both hurried off to our right and to the nearby back door of the peds ICU.

There was a flurry of activity over in room 4, and one of the nurses there looked over, saw me, and motioned for me to hurry.

I made my way to the side of the bed and looked down. It was Trish Sessions. One of the unit nurses had her hands around the girl's chest and was doing CPR, while another was pushing some IV medication through the tubing in her arm. Two of the staff pediatricians were standing at the foot of her bed, nervously looking at the various monitors on the wall and quietly conferring with each other.

"Is there anything I can do?" I asked them.

Trish had remained stable during the night, then had suddenly crashed a little over an hour ago. She lost her blood pressure and then her cardiac activity became very irregular. Her heart had been fibrillating for the past five minutes.

She was gone.

I didn't speak to John or Fay Sessions that morning. Their family doctor had come in and talked with them about Trish and about how it was an accident and no one's fault. And the doctor had stressed the importance of their supporting each other during this time and in the weeks and years to come.

Within six months they were divorced. It wasn't long after that I saw John in the ER. He had come in with some multiple and vague complaints. He told me about the divorce and that Fay had moved back to Georgia to be near her family.

John Sessions was only a shell of the man I had seen that terrible morning in the ER. He had the same vacant, troubled eyes, but now he was lost. I wanted desperately to help him, but this kind of pain was beyond my healing. He needed to find forgiveness. And then he needed to forgive himself.

Get Off My Bus

Robert, if it's under control when the 10 a.m. doctor comes in, Walter Stevens would like to meet with us in his office."

Virginia had walked up beside me at the nurses' station and spoke quietly, making sure no one heard what she said.

I looked up at the clock. That was a little less than an hour from now, and the morning hadn't been too bad.

"Okay, Virginia," I told her, signing the bottom of the chart in front of me and tossing it into the discharge basket. "I'll do what I can."

She turned without saying anything more and walked back to her office.

Great, I thought. *That's just what I need—another meeting with Walter Stevens.*

Darren walked up and put the chart of the patient in ENT on the countertop.

"This is a good one," he said, smiling.

Just then, I heard a loud holler from down the hallway in the direction of our ENT room.

"OH, LORDY!"

I looked down at the chart and asked him, "What's the problem? Why the—"

"OH, LORDY! DO SOMETHING!"

"She's got a bug in her ear," Darren explained. "Looks like a candle fly, and it's moving around. I thought I could grab it with some tweezers but it went in deeper. She thinks it's going to lay eggs in there, and that's really got her freaked out."

"Come on," I told him. "Let's go rescue this gal."

When Ted Nivens came in at ten, the bug lady was gone and there were only two other patients in the department. Virginia Granger was standing behind the counter. Her arms were folded across her chest and she was looking at me over the tops of her glasses.

"Looks like we can go now," she told me, stepping around Amy Connors and heading down the hallway. I told Ted where we would be and tried to catch up with her.

When we turned the corner and passed the entrance to X-ray, I asked her, "What do you think this is about, Virginia? More of Stevens's investigation?"

"I'm sure that's it," she said flatly. "He told me he had some definitive information and he wanted to share it with us."

"Definitive," I repeated, slowly stressing each syllable. "I wonder what that means."

She looked over at me and said, "Robert, let's just let him do the talking. We're only there to get information and see what he's thinking."

"Why do we have to deal with this guy? Why don't we just go directly to Bill Chalmers?"

Chalmers had been the hospital administrator for the past ten years, and I had always found him to be reasonable and focused on patient care. That always made things easier for us.

"I wanted to do that too," she answered. "But Bill made it clear we needed to deal with Stevens. Don't ask me why, but that's where we are."

We turned another corner and stood in front of the door to the administrative offices.

"Remember," Virginia said, looking me straight in my eyes. "Let him do the talking. And keep your temper. We both know how you can get sometimes."

"Virginia, I—" But she had already opened the door and walked into the administrative waiting area.

Walter Stevens was expecting us. He didn't stand up when we entered his office.

"Have a seat, Ms. Granger," he said to her, pointing to one of the chairs in front of his desk.

Then he pointed to the other chair. "Robert."

I quickly glanced around the room, noting the prominent display of diplomas on the wall behind him and the copy of the *Wall Street Journal* neatly folded on his large mahogany desk.

Something seemed odd however, and I looked over to Virginia to see if I was imagining this. I wasn't. She was sitting low to the floor like I was, and much lower than Stevens was behind his desk. This was textbook first-year business negotiation, or maybe Machiavelli 101. He was in an elevated position, and we were forced to look up at him. It was meant to intimidate the people you were meeting with, without their even knowing it. I glanced over again at Virginia. She cut her eyes at me, looked down briefly at her chair, and gave me a slight nod. I cleared my throat and shifted in my seat.

"Dr. Lesslie, Ms. Granger," Stevens began. "I'm glad you could meet with me this morning. I believe I have some interesting news for you, and something that should greatly relieve you."

He paused and put his palms flat on the top of his desk, surveying the two of us with apparent satisfaction. I wanted to say something but remembered Virginia's admonition. Between the two of them, I was much more afraid of our head nurse.

"Go on," she said to him.

He reached behind him to a small credenza and picked up a manila folder. I immediately recognized it as an employee file, but when he tossed it on his desk, there was no name on the outside.

Stevens began drumming on the chart with his fingers as he continued. "We've done some extensive research into your ER staff and have found some interesting evidence. In fact, I now know beyond the shadow of a doubt who has been stealing the drugs from your department. And while I don't know yet where they have been selling them, I know what they have been doing with the money."

"What in the—" I uttered, cut off by a sharp glance from Virginia.

As if he hadn't noticed my remark, Stevens went on. "You have a criminal in your department, Virginia, and it's time for them to be exposed and terminated. Well…" he paused, chuckling at himself. "Not really *terminated*, in the strictest sense. But they will lose their job immediately. And I intend to see that they are prosecuted to the fullest extent of the law. We will make an example of them so that this sort of thing never happens again."

He cleared his throat and settled back in his chair.

"You may have heard my theory of 'the bus,'" he continued. My ears perked up when he said this, and I thought I noticed Virginia shake her head, just a little.

"You see, the hospital is like a big bus, and it is the administration's responsibility to be sure we have the right people on board. We want Rock Hill General to be the best bus—the best hospital—it can be. And we know clearly that someone on our bus doesn't need to be here. It's my job to determine that and to collect the evidence needed to prove it."

He stopped and looked first at the head nurse and then at me. He was enjoying this and was waiting for our response. I stared at him and then at Virginia. She was amazingly calm, and just sat there quietly. Then slowly she brought her right hand up, adjusted her glasses, and put her index finger over her lips. I knew that look, and I knew she was getting angry.

"And just how have you collected this evidence, Walter?" she asked him quietly.

He leaned back in his chair and put his hands on the armrests.

"I'm afraid that is confidential," he told her gravely. "But ironclad, you can be sure of that. And Bill Chalmers is aware of my findings and is in full agreement with my plan of action."

Out of the corner of my eye I could see Virginia's shoulders slump a little. Her hand went back to her lap. For the first time, I was becoming discouraged.

We sat there, the three of us, and just looked at each other. It was clear to me that Walter Stevens was willing, if not eager, to sacrifice someone for his own gain. There was a malevolent streak in this man that made my skin crawl.

Finally, Stevens couldn't wait any longer.

"Don't you want to know who this is?" he asked, jabbing the file in front of him with his finger. "Don't you want to solve this matter and be done with it?"

Virginia just stared at him, and I didn't say a word.

"Well, you need to know," he declared, leaning forward in his chair and picking up the file. "Because tomorrow, we will be taking action."

He opened the folder, spun it around, and slid it across the desk in front of the two of us. I couldn't read anything in the record—it was still too far away. But attached to the left side of the chart, stapled to the upper left corner, was a black-and-white picture of the employee.

I felt as if someone had punched me in the gut. It was Amy Connors.

Ambushed

Virginia and I retraced our steps back to the ER, silent and shaken by what we had just learned. Stevens hadn't offered any further explanation, and after making it clear that the meeting was over, he instructed us not to tell anyone about his plans. He was going to meet with Amy Connors the next day and "handle things then."

Finally I looked over at Virginia and asked, "Well, what do you think of that?"

She abruptly stopped in the hallway and turned to face me.

"I think he's crazy," she said flatly. "He doesn't have any idea what he's talking about. You and I have both known Amy for more than ten years, and if there's anyone in the department I would trust with my life, it would be her. Stealing drugs and selling them? Preposterous! Or stealing the drugs and using them herself? That's insane! I wanted to reach over and grab him by his neck and shake him for everything he's worth…which wouldn't be much!"

Suddenly, I had of vision of her doing this, and I couldn't keep myself from smiling.

"Don't you laugh at me!" she huffed, then turned and started off again for the ER.

I caught up with her long strides and said, "After hearing all that, don't you think we need to go to Bill Chalmers? I mean, this is so off the wall, I think he ought to know about it."

"I'm going to do just that, this afternoon," she told me with determination. "But I'm a little concerned. Bill made it clear how he wanted to handle this, and he may not be willing to listen. But he's got to know what Stevens is up to, and I know he doesn't want to lose one of the best secretaries in the whole hospital."

We had turned the corner into the department and stopped outside the empty ortho room.

"This business about us not telling anybody," I said quietly. "I'm not sure if that's—"

"What business are you talking about?" she asked with a straight face.

"You know, the—"

"I didn't hear anything like that," she interrupted. "In fact, I'm going to sit down with Amy right now. She needs to know what's going on, and she needs to know where I stand on this before Stevens gets hold of her."

She was about to walk up the hall, when she added, "You can sit down with us too, if you want. In fact, that might be a good idea."

Things were happening quickly and I was still trying to get my head around what Stevens had told us. But of course I would sit down with the two of them. I didn't want Amy to think I had any part in this.

I followed Virginia up the hallway to the nurses' station, where she stopped, leaned over the counter, and said something to Amy.

Ted came out of room 1 and walked over to me.

"Well, how did *that* go?" he asked me, knowing only that we had met with one of the administrators. "Anything serious going on?"

He put his chart down on the counter and started making some notes, obviously not too concerned.

"Just some of the usual," I told him. Once things were out in the open, I would make sure he knew everything that was going on.

"Yeah, I know how that goes," he replied, not looking up from his work. Then speaking to Lori Davidson, he said, "Lori, the guy in 1 needs a urine and a CBC." He handed her the chart and added, "Thanks, and let me know when it's back."

The countertop was empty, with no patient charts to be picked up.

"I'm going back to the lounge for some coffee," he told me. "Want a cup?"

"No, I'm fine," I answered, watching Virginia and Amy step into the head nurse's office. "I'll be with Virginia if you need me."

"Okay. I'll be right back. There's not much cookin' right now." He headed down the hallway, and I walked over to Virginia's office.

Amy glanced over at me as the door closed. She was sitting in one of the chairs across from Virginia, and I walked over and sat down beside her. She looked first at the head nurse, then at me, and then back to Virginia.

"What's up?" she asked, smiling. "Did I win the lottery? Or am I in some kind of trouble?"

Virginia glanced over at me and then quickly back at Amy.

"We need to talk about something," she began, taking off her glasses and carefully placing them on the desk. "And this is awkward for me, Amy. In fact, I can't believe we have to have this conversation. But there are a few things you need to know."

She cleared her throat and looked over at me. Amy turned her head and also looked at me, her eyes searching mine, the smile now gone from her face.

"You two are spookin' me," she said. "Why so serious? Have I done somethin' wrong? Or has somethin' happened to Charlie or the…"

She grabbed the arms of her chair and was about to stand up when Virginia said, "No, no, Amy. Nothing like that. Charlie and your children are fine. This has nothing to do with them."

Amy slowly sat back down in her chair, relieved, but still confused. "Then what is this about?" she asked.

The head nurse took a deep breath and began. "I'm sure you've heard that we've had some medications missing in the department. First some noncontrolled drugs, and now narcotics."

Amy nodded her head and said, "Yeah, I've heard a little about that. A couple of the nurses were talkin' about it the other day, but what does that have to do with me? I don't have any idea about where that stuff might have gone or who might have gotten it. I don't know how I can help you with it."

Virginia picked up her glasses and started cleaning them with some Kleenex.

Amy looked over at me again. When I looked away, I saw her stiffen a little.

The head nurse put her glasses back on and looked at Amy. Before she could say anything Amy exclaimed, "Wait a minute! Do you think I know somethin' about this? I just told you I barely heard about it the other day. Nobody has told me anything!"

"Amy, it's not that," Virginia explained quietly, trying to calm the young secretary. "I'm afraid it's much worse."

The secretary slumped in her chair and stared at her.

"Worse? What do you mean 'worse'?" she asked, stunned.

Virginia told her about our conversation with Walter Stevens, and about his being convinced that not only did our secretary know about the missing drugs, but that she was the one stealing them. I was struck once again by the absurdity of this whole idea, and yet here we were, telling Amy and confronting her with what the administration was determined to do.

When Virginia finished, Amy stood up and headed for the door.

"Amy!" I said, turning quickly. "Where are you going?"

She stopped and spun around, fixing us with a look of anger and hurt.

"I'm going right to Mr. Chalmers and set things straight!" she told us defiantly. "This is the craziest thing I've ever heard, and I'm not goin' to stand for it! Dr. Lesslie, Ms. Granger, you know I'm not involved with this! How could they even begin to think I would do somethin' like this?"

She was silent, and looked first at Virginia and then at me. Suddenly her shoulders slumped and there was a look of confusion on her face, and then there was that same hurt.

"You guys don't…" she muttered.

Virginia jumped up from her chair and hurried over to Amy. She put an arm around her and led her back to her seat.

"Of course we don't think you have anything to do with this," she told her. "This came out of the clear blue at us, and we haven't had time to think about the best way to deal with it. But we wanted to talk with you and let you know what was happening."

"We didn't want you to be blindsided," I said, turning in my chair so I was facing her directly. "We're going to figure this out, and knock some sense into Walter Stevens if we can."

"If Charlie finds out about this, he'll be knockin' more than the *sense* out of that little jerk," she said, trying to force a smile.

"Anyway, Amy," Virginia continued. "If you want to take the rest of the day off, I'll understand. We'll get someone to cover. I'm going to leave that up to you. But whatever you decide to do, I must ask you not to mention this to anyone, not even Charlie. We're not supposed to be telling you this, but thought you needed to know."

"I thought you didn't hear that part," I needled Virginia.

"Oh hush, Dr. Lesslie," she said, not looking at me. "But Amy, we've given you a lot to handle, and if you need to—"

"I'll be fine, Ms. Granger," the secretary said, sitting up straighter in her chair and beginning to collect herself. "I need to work, and I'll be alright." Then with trust and pleading in her eyes, she looked at each of us in turn and said, "But I'm counting on you guys to help me."

After she left the office, I said, "Virginia, are you sure we don't need to go talk with Bill Chalmers right now? I think it might do some good."

She thought for a moment, then answered me. "I think I've changed my mind, Dr. Lesslie. We should wait before we talk with Bill. Let's just let this play out. We need to see what kind of *evidence* Walter has, if any. Personally, I think this is a bunch of hot air, and he doesn't have anything. His preoccupation with Amy will blow over, and then we'll still have to find out who is doing this. I know you're impatient to get this done with, but if we give Walter a little rope, maybe he'll take care of hanging himself."

"I just don't want to see Amy get hurt any more than she already is," I told her, not yet convinced about her change of plan. I still thought Chalmers might be able to get Stevens under control and off Amy's back. In the end though, I yielded to Virginia's wisdom.

"I guess we'll wait and see what happens tomorrow," I acquiesced.

"Yep," was all she said.

I got up and walked to the door. My hand was on the doorknob when Virginia spoke. "Dr. Lesslie, tell me, how is Darren Adler doing?"

Turning around, I noticed the look of concern on her face. Was something going on that I didn't know about? I told her what Ted

Nivens had shared with me, about his blowing up with the nurses in the CCU. But I couldn't think of anything else.

"Sounds like they deserved it," she responded, her face softening a little. "Is that it?"

I thought for another minute. "No, I think he's doing fine. He's always on time and he makes good decisions. He's great out in triage."

That was one of the toughest areas to work, and if you could handle triage effectively, you could handle anything in the department.

"Hmm…" she mused.

I knew where she was going and I was conflicted. I didn't think there was any way Darren was stealing drugs. I had known him for too many years and would never suspect him of doing something like this. He was headstrong, and sometimes that got him in trouble. But this— this was something totally different. Yet there was no way in the world it was Amy Connors. So *could* it be Darren? Was there a side of him I just couldn't see? No, it had to be someone else.

"I know what you're thinking," she said quietly. "And I can't imagine that Darren is involved. I just wish he were a little more laid-back, at least for the time being."

"If that's a suggestion, Virginia, I'll talk with him."

"It's a suggestion," she said, picking up a stack of papers, signaling the end of this conversation.

The rest of the day was uneventful, other than the awkwardness of interacting with Amy. I had to admire the way she was able to put this aside and do her job. But I knew that just under the surface her emotions were boiling. She and I were a lot alike. And I would be looking forward to my confrontation with Walter Stevens. There wouldn't be a lot of pleasantries exchanged between the two of us.

13

Dangerous Assumptions

6:58 a.m. On the way to the hospital the next morning, my mind was spinning with what might transpire between Amy and Walter Stevens. As I walked through the ambulance entrance, I was surprised to see she wasn't sitting behind the counter of the nurses' station. She should have been here by now. Instead, it was Susan Everett, the night-shift secretary.

I was about to ask her about Amy, when we heard loud screaming from down the hallway.

"Ortho," Susan said calmly. "Dr. Kennick's in there with some guy from Chester. Sammy Hodges, twenty-seven-year-old," she commented, looking down at a folder. "The ER doc sent him here 'cause he couldn't get his shoulder back in place, or somethin' like that."

I turned and was headed toward the orthopedic room, when Susan called out, "Oh, and Amy will be a little late this morning. She's having trouble with her truck."

I was greeted by another loud cry of pain as I stepped through the doorway of ortho. There, in the far corner of the room, was the source of all of this commotion.

Sammy Hodges was lying on one of the stretchers. He looked over as I approached his bed, and his eyes became big as saucers.

"Arggh!" he bellowed, thrashing around but unable to escape Liz Kennick's attempts at putting his shoulder back in place. She had Sammy's left wrist firmly in her grasp and was applying traction to his left shoulder. One of our male techs stood on the other side of the stretcher, fiercely gripping the ends of a sheet that was passed under Sammy's back, under his armpit, and back over his chest. The sheet was serving as a countertraction to what Liz was doing.

The first thing that struck me was the red faces of everyone in the room. Sammy's face was red and contorted in obvious pain. The tech's face was also red, and he was sweating. He was a big guy and was pulling with all his strength, making sure that the patient's torso didn't move an inch. And there was Liz, huffing and puffing and tugging for all she was worth. She looked up at me as I approached the bed.

"Robert, this is a tough one!" she gasped.

"What have you got?" I asked her, looking over at the X-ray view box. Its light was off and there were no films hanging on it.

"The ER doc over in Chester called me a little while ago. Mr. Hodges here apparently fell and injured his left shoulder sometime during the night. He's not sure how it happened, but he went to the ER over there and they told him he had a dislocation. They tried for about an hour to get it back in place, but couldn't. So they sent him over here to see one of the orthopedists. I thought I'd try to get it back in before bothering one of them."

She leaned back a little more, putting greater pressure on Sammy's shoulder.

"Arggh!" he yelled again, looking up at me for help.

"Have you given him anything for pain?" I asked, stepping around so I could examine Sammy's shoulder.

"Yeah, we started an IV and he's had 5 of morphine. Doesn't seem to have touched him, though, and I'm probably going to need to give him some more."

"He may need a good bit more than that," I said, gently palpating his upper arm and shoulder. He was very muscular, making it more difficult to accurately feel his landmarks. It also made it more difficult to overcome any muscle spasm and return the head of the humerus to its socket.

"Are you sure he's still out of joint?" I asked her, puzzled because I thought I could feel the head where it was supposed to be.

"Yes," she answered without hesitation. "It's an anterior dislocation and it's still out. Textbook case, with a squaring off of the shoulder and everything. I just need to keep applying traction and it should pop back in place. Would you ask one of the nurses to come back here with more morphine?"

"Sure," I answered, heading to the door. "Did they send some films with him?" I asked, looking around again for an X-ray folder.

"Yes," she said. "I think they're up at the nurses' station. Maybe behind the counter."

"Good—I'll be right back."

"Arggh!" Sammy screamed again, causing me to cringe a little as I walked up the hallway.

Virginia was standing at the nurses' station, looking over Susan's shoulder and pointing to something in the logbook. She looked up as I walked around the counter.

"What's going on back there?" she asked. "Sounds like someone's having his gallbladder removed without anesthesia."

"It does, doesn't it?" I agreed. I told her what was going on and that I was looking for Sammy Hodges's X-rays.

"I think they're over there," Susan said, spinning around in her chair and pointing to the back counter. "Dr. Kennick put them down there when he came in."

"Thanks," I told her, walking over and picking up the folder.

Chester County Hospital, the jacket read. Under that was Sammy's name, date of birth, and *Left shoulder—2 views.*

I stepped over to the view box, took the films out of the jacket, and snapped them into place. Virginia walked up beside me as I switched on the light.

"Oh no!" I exclaimed, not believing my eyes. I grabbed the X-rays, stepped around our head nurse, and took off for the ortho room.

"What's wrong?" Virginia called after me. "What is it?"

"It's not what she thinks it is!" I called back to her over my shoulder.

Racing to the room and over to the stretcher, I stopped right beside Liz and said, "Hold on, and don't pull on his shoulder anymore!"

"I've almost got it," she objected. "I felt something move a little just a second ago, and I think with—"

"Don't pull on him anymore!"

Without waiting for her to respond, I reached down and took his hand in mine. "Here, let me hold this a minute," I told him.

Liz backed away, puzzled, and looked up at me.

"Can I let go?"

It was the tech on the other side of the stretcher. He was exhausted and breathing hard.

"Yes," I told him. "You can let go of that sheet."

He thankfully complied and leaned back against the wall.

"Robert, what in the world—"

"Come over here with me," I said to her, while gently placing Sammy's arm across his chest. "Here," I told him. "Keep your arm just like this. I think it will feel better."

He had closed his eyes and was nodding his head in obvious relief.

I looked up at the tech and said, "Make sure he keeps his arm just like that, okay?"

"Sure thing, Doc," he replied.

Liz followed me over to the view box on the wall just to the right of the doorway. I put Sammy's films up and flipped the switch.

"What do you think about that?" I asked her, intentionally not pointing out the obvious pathology.

She studied the X-rays for a moment, her eyebrows scrunched in deliberate and focused concentration. Then suddenly her eyes opened wide and she mumbled, "Oh, Lord!"

She moved a little closer, carefully studying Sammy's shoulder joint. He didn't have a dislocation. In fact, he had never had a dislocation. It was something altogether different.

Slowly, almost painfully, Liz's index finger approached the view box and came to rest over Sammy's A-C joint. That was where the problem lay. The X-rays from Chester showed a complete A-C separation, *not* a dislocation. The ER doc in Chester had missed it, and Liz hadn't looked at it.

"Robert, I…" she stammered.

I didn't say anything, but waited for her to verbalize her thoughts.

"Have I hurt this man?" she whispered, shaking her head. "I've been pulling hard on that shoulder, and…If I've made it worse, I'll…"

"I don't think you hurt his A-C joint any more than the initial injury," I told her. "Or any more than the ER doc down in Chester did. But you certainly caused him more pain than he should have had."

"Good Lord," she continued in a hushed voice. "I need to go tell him, and apologize. I should have looked at these films first, before doing anything."

"You're right about that," I agreed, not willing to let her off the hook, but also not wanting to let her beat herself up too much. She needed to learn from this, and I thought she was getting the lesson.

We walked back over to our patient's stretcher, and I explained to him what was wrong with his shoulder and that one of the orthopedists would be coming down to see him. Then Liz apologized, a couple of times.

"It's okay, Miss," he told her through the haze of the additional morphine we had given him. "If you weren't so purty, I might be upset."

As we walked up the hall, Liz asked me, "Are you sure he's going to be alright? I didn't cause any permanent damage, did I?"

"No," I answered truthfully. "He's going to be fine. He'll need surgery, but that was true from the moment he first injured himself. The important thing here, though, is that we learn something from it."

"I know, I know," she said. "Never make assumptions."

"You're absolutely right," I agreed. "That's one of the main things that get ER doctors—*any* doctors—in trouble. When we start assuming things, we're usually headed down the wrong road."

"I should have looked at those films for myself," she responded, shaking her head again. "But that doc sounded so sure of the dislocation, and it seemed like he knew what he was talking about, and—"

"And you *assumed*," I interrupted.

"Yes, I assumed," she said in resignation.

We had reached the nurses' station and I said, "Have you got a minute, or are you too tired?"

"I'm wide awake now," she answered, taking a deep breath and looking up at me.

"Come over here then," I told her. "I want to tell you something."

We walked over to the back counter, pulled up two chairs, and sat down.

"I know you need to get out of here," I began, glancing up at the clock on the wall. "But this is important, and it's something to learn early on. I guess the best way to make this point is to give you an example of how things can go bad."

"I think things went pretty bad back in ortho," she interjected. "That's an example right there."

"It *is* an example," I agreed. "But let me tell you how things can really get twisted, and people can get hurt. Sammy's going to do fine, but that's not always the case."

Liz settled in her chair, folded her arms, and looked at me expectantly.

"You've met Nolan Bridges, I think."

"The family practitioner from Fort Mill?" she asked.

I nodded, and she said, "Yes, he's come through the ER a couple of times. Nice guy."

"Yeah, he's a nice guy," I agreed. "Not long after we moved to Rock Hill, I saw a fifty- or sixty-year-old man in the ER—came in with cough and some congestion. I can't remember his name, but he looked fine. No fever, no chest pain, no shortness of breath, just a cough for a couple of days. Sounded straightforward to me."

"Bronchitis," Liz opined.

"That's what I thought," I said. "And I gave him an antibiotic and something for his cough and told him to follow up with his family doctor if he wasn't better in a few days. That was Dr. Bridges, and he saw him a week or so later, no better with his cough. Still no fever, just the congestion. And the cough was keeping him awake at night. Bridges saw him and gave him a different antibiotic. This time he was wheezing a little, so he gave him an inhaler too."

"That all sounds reasonable," Liz said. "But I don't see the connection with Sammy Hodges. How does that—"

"Just hold on," I stopped her. "Bridges saw him two or three more times in the office with the same complaints and kept changing things around. Put him on some steroids, and that seemed to help a little. But the cough never went away. Then one night he showed up in the ER. I remembered him from a couple of weeks earlier, and he told me what had been going on. He was wheezing that night, and seemed a little short of breath. Still no fever or chest pain, and he looked okay. I was about to treat him again for a persistent bronchitis, but something just didn't seem right. I got a chest X-ray, and guess what?"

"Pneumonia!" Liz exclaimed, satisfied that she had solved this case.

"No, it wasn't pneumonia," I told her, my eyes searching hers for another response.

"Not pneumonia?" she responded, frustrated. "Well, what was it?" she asked, giving up.

"This man had early heart failure," I said. "And he'd had it for a couple of weeks. I didn't pick up on it when he first came to the ER, and then Bridges made the assumption that I knew what I was talking about."

"That's a big assumption," she chuckled. "But this wasn't a straightforward presentation of heart failure."

"Doesn't matter," I said. "The point here is that a string of assumptions—his assuming my diagnosis was correct, and then my assuming his diagnosis was correct, and then his assuming my diagnosis was correct..."

"Okay, okay—I get it!" she laughed. "Never make assumptions!"

"That *is* the point," I agreed. "But you can see how subtle this can be. It's an easy trap to fall into, especially in the ER. The safest thing to do is always step back, take a look at things, and don't be lazy. Sometimes the toughest course is the right one. No, that's not true. *Usually* the toughest course is the right one."

Liz was thinking about this last statement, and I was about to tell her about Miles Sudderth, when I looked up again at the clock. It was 7:45 and she needed to get out of here and get some sleep. I told her just that, and she was soon up and on her way home.

"And next time," I called out to her, "We'll talk about why you shouldn't believe everything you see or everything a patient tells you."

As she walked through the ambulance entrance, the orthopedist on call passed her on his way in to see Sammy Hodges.

I was still sitting at the back counter wondering when Amy Connors would make it to work, and I found myself thinking about Miles Sudderth again. That had been a close one.

It had happened a long time ago, just a year or so after I had finished my residency. Jack Frazier, a friend of mine who was two years behind me in the emergency medicine training program was moonlighting in a small ER, not far from here. It was a fall weekend afternoon, and I remember the day as being perfect. Because it was a "football Saturday" the afternoon hours in the ER were typically quiet. That would probably change in the evening.

Sometime around 3 p.m., Jack called me.

"Robert, I'm over here at Divine Savior and I've got a fifty-two-year-old man I need to send your way."

Divine Savior was a small hospital, its doors long closed now, and it had a minimal capacity for handling emergencies. Fortunately, most people in the area bypassed it on their way to Rock Hill General, but every once in a while they would get some really sick or injured patients.

"Tell me about him," I said, taking my pen in hand and sliding a pad of paper in front of me.

"I think it's going to be straightforward," he began. "His name is Miles Sudderth, and he started having chest pain about an hour ago. He only lives a half mile from the hospital, so he came here instead of driving over to Rock Hill. Blood pressure's a little high—160/110—and he takes medicine for that. No diabetes, but he used to smoke."

I heard him talking to someone in the background and then he continued.

"His EKG is abnormal—looks like an acute anterior MI, with big changes in those leads. But like I said, his pressure's not low, and he doesn't seem to be in any distress right now. Still with some chest pain, but we're giving him some nitro for that now, and then some morphine. His chest X-ray looks good to me, but there's no radiologist over here to show it to."

So far, it *did* sound straightforward. Jack was a good resident and was always on top of things. I had no reason to believe that anything he was telling me wasn't accurate.

We talked a little more and then made arrangements for Sudderth's transfer to Rock Hill General.

"We'll be expecting him," I told Jack. "What do you think, maybe twenty minutes?"

"That's sounds about right," he answered. "And give me a call when you get a chance and let me know how he's doing. He's a nice guy, and his whole family is here with him. I'm working a '24,' so you'll know where to find me."

Betty Caldwell was the nurse working with me, and I called her over and told her what was coming in.

"I'll give Pete Jenkins a call and let him know too," I told her.

Jenkins was the first cardiologist to come to Rock Hill, and that had only been about six months earlier. He was well-trained, energetic, and determined that Rock Hill General would be on the cutting edge when it came to hearts and community hospitals. I was glad to have him available.

"And Betty," I added. "Get the TPA ready in cardiac. It sounds like we might be using it."

These were the early days of the "clot-busters," those medications used to dissolve blood clots that formed in the vessels of the heart, causing heart attacks. TPA was one of the early ones, and we had it stocked in the ER, ready for use. These drugs were capable of saving peoples' lives, but they could be dangerous as well.

I called Pete Jenkins and told him what was going on.

"If it looks like an acute MI, get the TPA started as fast as you can," he responded. "I'll be right in."

As I hung up the phone, Miles Sudderth came through the ambulance entrance on his stretcher. I introduced myself to him as he passed the nurses' station, and took his chart and X-ray folder from one of the paramedics.

"Over here," Betty called out from the doorway of cardiac.

I opened Sudderth's folder and spread out his paperwork on the countertop. A quick look at his EKG confirmed what Jack had told me. The pattern was classic for an acute heart attack. I quickly scanned the rest of his record, but found nothing significant. Then I picked up his X-ray folder, took out the single film, and walked over to the view box.

It looked fine. His lungs were clear, and his heart shape and size were normal. I peered closer at the X-ray, searching for a subtle partially collapsed lung. I didn't want to miss that.

Nothing. Everything on his chest film looked good.

When I walked into cardiac, Sudderth had already been moved over to our stretcher, and his IV line and oxygen tubing were being adjusted.

"How do you feel?" I asked him. "Are you still having any chest pain?"

I glanced over at his monitor—his heart rate was 82, nice and regular.

"150 over 100," Betty told me, taking her stethoscope out of her ears and putting it down on the counter behind me.

"I'm still having some pain, Dr. Lesslie," he told me. "Not as bad as when I first got to Divine Savior, but it's still there."

He was pointing to the middle of his chest and was moving a little on the stretcher, trying to get comfortable.

The two paramedics from EMS were packing up their equipment, getting ready to leave.

"I think Dr. Frazier gave him another 5 of morphine right before we left," one of them said. "That's a total of 15 he's had."

"Thanks," I said as the men rolled their stretcher out of the room. That was a pretty good dose of morphine, and along with the nitroglycerin, he should be having some relief. This was even more reason to get the TPA going and try to open up his coronary vessels.

"Betty, how close are we with the TPA?" I asked her.

"Just about ready," she answered, with her back to me. She was standing at the counter, preparing the medication. It was a simple white powder that had to be mixed with saline, and it was expensive—more than two thousand dollars a dose.

Just don't drop it! I thought.

In another minute or so, she had the TPA ready to be infused through one of Sudderth's IVs. I explained to him what we were going to do, what we wanted to see happen, and what he might feel. I also told him there was some risk involved, and that a small number of people had hemorrhages in their heads from the medication. He didn't fall into any of the high-risk groups, but it was still a possibility.

"Is this the best thing for me, Dr. Lesslie?" he asked me, still rubbing the middle of his chest. "I mean, if you were me lying here, would you take the TPA?"

That question always made me stop and think. After all, that should be one of the things that guide our actions. Would I take the same treatments that I offer my patients?

"Mr. Sudderth, this is exactly what I would do," I told him confidently. "And I would do it right now."

He nodded his head slowly and looked away.

"Okay then—let's do it," he said quietly.

"Dr. Lesslie," Betty said from the other side of the stretcher. "Would you check this for me?"

She was taking his blood pressure again, this time in his right arm.

A little impatiently, I walked around the bed to where she stood.

"I just checked his pressure and it's 180 over 110 in this arm," she informed me. "Would you see what you get? That's a lot higher than in his left."

I quickly felt the pulse in his right wrist and then compared it to his left. They seemed about the same, and his hands were warm. But sometimes you can't detect subtle changes, even not-so-subtle ones. I needed to check the blood pressure in both arms.

Betty was right. His BP on the right side was 180/112. I quickly stepped to the other side of the stretcher and checked his left arm. 140/96. Something was wrong.

The door opened and Pete Jenkins walked into the room.

"Hey, Robert," he greeted me, then nodded his head at Mr. Sudderth. "I looked at the EKG out on the counter, and I agree with you. He's having an MI. And if that's his chest X-ray on the view box, it looks okay. Have you started the TPA yet?"

Betty had walked over to the IV stand and was getting ready to start the infusion.

"Hold on!" I told her, holding up my hand. "Pete, we've got a problem here. I'm not sure this is an MI," I told him. "There's a difference in the pressures between his arms, and I think we need an echocardiogram, stat."

Pete walked over to the stretcher and checked the pulses in Sudderth's wrists, and then his legs. He had a puzzled look on his face, having felt the same warm extremities I had.

"What are the differences?" he asked, picking up Betty's clipboard and scanning it for the patient's vital signs. "Wow!" he exclaimed when he saw the measurements.

We had an echocardiogram done in the room, and Pete studied its screen, pointing out to me the source of Miles Sudderth's chest pain.

It wasn't a heart attack after all, at least not the type we were getting ready to treat. He had a dissection of his aorta. The layers of the biggest blood vessel in his body were coming apart and separating. But instead of extending away from his heart and down into his chest, the dissection had traveled back toward his heart. As it had reached the blood vessels that feed the heart muscle, it had sheared them off, effectively blocking them just like a blood clot would have.

But his problem wasn't a blood clot, and had we given him the TPA, he could easily have bled out and died.

"We're not going to be giving him the TPA," Pete told Betty.

Then he looked down at our patient and said, "Mr. Sudderth, you're going to need surgery, and soon."

That had been a close one—too close. And it was a lesson I had never forgotten.

I stood up and stretched, looked around the department, and then walked over to the other side of the nurses' station. Standing in front of Susan Everett, I asked her, "Any word from our missing secretary?"

"I'm comin' as fast as I can!"

It was Amy Connors, hurrying up the hallway from the staff lounge.

"I got here as quick as I could," she said, walking around the counter and waiting for Susan to get up out of her chair. "Wouldn't you know it? A brand-new truck, and the battery's dead."

The phone rang and Susan picked it up. She listened for a moment, then handed it to Amy.

"It's for you," she told her. "Walter Stevens."

Caught in the Web

A my looked up at me. There was a cold resolution in her eyes, and I nodded my head, understanding her need to get this over with.

Susan reached under the desk, grabbed her purse, and stood up.

"It's all yours," she told Amy, oblivious to the emotional turmoil surrounding her.

"Do you want me to stay over tonight?" Amy asked her. "I really appreciate you hanging around for me."

"No, don't worry about that," Susan answered, smiling. "You've done it for me enough times. And probably will again."

She walked around the counter and down the hallway, leaving me alone with Amy.

"Any advice?" she asked me.

"Just what Virginia always tells me," I answered. "Let him do the talking. If you wait long enough, he'll show all his cards and then you can respond. You don't need to tell him much of anything 'cause he doesn't have much of anything. And try to keep your cool."

Once again, we were a lot alike, and I knew this last request would be difficult for her.

"I'll do my best," she said, moving around the counter and stepping over in front of room 5. "I'll be back as fast as I can. And if you hear a Code Blue, well…it won't be *me* needin' CPR."

I chuckled at this, knowing she was right, but a little worried because she *was* right. As she disappeared down the hall, Virginia stepped out of her office and over to the nurses' station.

"Is she going to be okay?" she asked, nodding her head in the direction of the now empty corridor, but not really expecting an answer.

"This whole thing makes me sick," I told her. "I just wish one of us could be there with her. Stevens can be overbearing, as you well know."

"I'm just glad her husband didn't come with her," Virginia mused. "I actually had that thought as I was driving in this morning. Now *that* would be fireworks! But I don't think she said anything to him, because knowing Charlie, he wouldn't let her be doing this on her own if he knew about it. And then there would be trouble."

Jeff Ryan walked out of triage, leading a middle-aged man dressed in the garb of one of the city's utility workers. He was holding a bloody bandage to his right eyebrow, and the two of them headed toward minor trauma.

"Looks like you've got work to do," Virginia said, turning and walking back to her office.

Forty-five minutes later, Amy returned to the ER. I was standing at the nurses' station, talking with one of our surgeons about a ten-year-old in room 4 with a probable hot appendix. He would be heading to the OR shortly, and when I saw Amy coming up the hallway, I cut short my conversation. I could tell she was upset.

"Thanks, Robert," the surgeon said to me. "I'll let you know what we find."

He walked back over to room 4 as Amy passed behind him and over to her chair. Instead of sitting down, she reached under the counter and grabbed her book bag. Her face was flushed and she hadn't looked at me yet.

"Amy," I said tentatively. There was no response, and I repeated myself. "Amy?"

She raised her hand to silence me, and still wouldn't meet my eyes. Without saying a word, she stepped around the counter and headed for the ambulance entrance.

"Amy," I said again, trying to stop her or at least get her attention. She didn't answer and kept walking toward the exit.

Virginia Granger stepped out of the medicine room and saw Amy disappear through the automatic doors. The look on her face changed quickly from one of questioning to one of determination. She gestured with her head, indicating I was to follow Amy. I did, with Virginia right behind me.

Amy was walking quickly, almost running, and we were having trouble keeping up with her.

"Amy!" I called out. "Hold on a minute!"

She kept right on walking and didn't turn around.

"Amy, I need to talk with you!"

It was Virginia, and I had never heard this tone in her voice. She wasn't ordering her, or directing her secretary to do something. She was pleading with her to stop.

Amy did. And with her back still to us, she dropped her head to her chest. We caught up with her and she slowly turned around to face us.

"Amy, tell us what happened," the head nurse asked, coming up beside her. "What's the matter?"

She was staring down at the cracked pavement, silent and brooding. Then she looked up, first at me, then at Virginia.

"He fired me, that's what happened." She was blunt, almost accusatory.

"He did what?" I exclaimed, not believing what I had just heard.

Virginia reached out and put a hand on Amy's arm. She didn't pull away.

"Tell us what happened with Walter Stevens."

She recoiled at the sound of his name, and it took a moment or two for her to collect herself.

"I went in his office and sat down, and he immediately started in on me," she began, anger rising in her voice.

Virginia crossed her arms and started tapping her right foot, trying to control her own boiling emotions. "Take your time, Amy. Just take a deep breath and take your time."

She took a deep breath, blew it out, and looked straight into my eyes.

"He didn't waste any time," she began to tell us. "He told me he knew I had been stealing the drugs in the ER and he had proof. He wanted me to confess and get it over with."

"What kind of proof did he have?" I asked her, becoming angrier myself.

"He didn't have *any*, of course," Amy answered tersely. "I asked him the same thing, but he just hemmed and hawed and said I needed to confess and clear things up. I told him to go jump and that I hadn't done anything." That really teed him off, 'cause he got up out of his chair and started pacin' around the room."

"Amy," I interrupted her. "I told you to try to keep quiet and let him talk."

Virginia shot me a disapproving glance.

"I tried, Dr. Lesslie, but he's such an arrogant…an arrogant…" She glanced over at Virginia, not wanting to offend her.

"He's an arrogant jerk," Virginia said, finishing her sentence. "Go on."

"Then he pulled out a notepad and started going down some list he had made. He knew about our new truck and asked where we had got the money to buy it. I told him we had a car loan and that we were probably goin' to lose it, but he just blew that off. And he knew about Charlie losing his job."

"Charlie lost his job?" Virginia exclaimed, surprised by this news. "Amy, you didn't tell me about that."

Amy looked down at the pavement again and said, "It happened a couple of weeks ago. There were some layoffs at the plant, and Charlie was one of them. They promised he would be hired back on once things got better. But it's been tough, and I didn't want anybody to know about it. I didn't want you guys to worry about us."

"Amy…" Virginia said quietly.

"And he knew about us takin' Benji out of the private school. I don't know how he found out about that, but it really ticked me off. We wanted him to go out to Westminster and be with some of his friends, but when things got tight, we just couldn't…we couldn't afford it. Stevens said all those things pointed to 'motive' or something like that. He started talkin' about 'need' and 'opportunity' and about rationalizin' stuff, and I wanted to slug him."

"It's a good thing you didn't," I told her, trying to lighten the mood a little.

"How do you know I didn't?" she asked, staring straight at me with a serious expression on her face.

I flinched a little and she said, "Don't worry. I didn't slug him. Wanted to, but I didn't."

"You said he fired you," Virginia asked her. "How did that come about?"

"Well, first he told me to resign and be done with it," Amy began again. "When I told him that wasn't happenin', he told me that South Carolina was a 'hire at will' state, or somethin' like that, and that he could fire me for no cause. Just like that. Then he kept tryin' to get me to resign, telling me that it would look better on my record, and I would have a better chance of gettin' another job, and stuff like that. But I kept tellin' him I wasn't goin' to resign because I hadn't done anything wrong. That set him off all over again, and he started poundin' on his desk. I wanted to pound it with his head, but I didn't. Then all of a sudden, he stood up straight, took a deep breath, and got real calm. That's when I got nervous. Then he started talkin' about some *bus* and how I didn't need to be on it."

I glanced over at Virginia. She was shaking her head.

Amy stopped talking and looked again at each of us.

"Then he told me you two knew all about this and that you agreed with everything he was saying, and that you wanted me to resign too."

There was hurt in her voice and in her eyes.

"That's absurd!" Virginia snapped out, stepping closer to Amy. "We knew about this—that's why we talked with you yesterday. But neither of us believes a word of what Walter Stevens is saying, and we certainly don't want you to resign!"

"Well, it's too late for that," she said, pulling back a little from Virginia. "Like I said, he fired me. When I refused to resign, he said, 'Fine, then. Have it your way. You're fired and you are to leave the premises immediately.' Just like that. Then he told me to leave his office. I had more to say to him, but he said 'Just get out,' and that's what I did. I'm done with this place," she said, looking over at the hospital and shaking her head.

"Done with it," she repeated. Then she turned and started off again toward her truck.

"Amy!" I called after her.

She raised her hand in the air and kept walking. I looked over at Virginia and she shook her head, silencing me.

"We have to give her some time," she said quietly. "A little space is what she needs right now."

"Well, she might need some space, Virginia," I told her. "But I'm going to see Bill Chalmers."

Once again, Virginia Granger would prove to be right. When I had a break, I went to the administration offices and asked the secretary there if I could speak with Bill Chalmers. The waiting area was surrounded by four or five offices, one for the CEO and the others for various vice presidents. The door to Walter Stevens's office was the only one open and I could see him sitting behind his desk. He was looking away from me, leaning back in his chair with his feet up on his desk, talking on the phone. He was animated, and he was smiling. That almost did it for me. It was all I could do to keep from charging into his office and letting him have it, but that wouldn't do Amy any good. I took a deep breath and looked away.

"Mr. Chalmers will see you now, Dr. Lesslie," his secretary politely told me.

"Thanks," I said, then walked over to his closed door.

I rapped on the paneled wood, and then stepped into his office. Chalmers was sitting behind his desk. He stood up, walked over to me, and shook my hand.

"Have a seat, Robert," he told me, gesturing to a couple of chairs clustered around a small coffee table. I could tell he had been expecting this visit. I sat down and he took the chair beside me.

Bill Chalmers and I had always gotten along. I respected him, even liked him, which was a little unusual, considering the constant potential for conflict between a hospital administrator and his medical staff.

Bill was a businessman and he knew the importance of the bottom line, and of keeping the hospital operating in the black. But unlike too many hospital administrators, he also knew the importance of providing the best medical care possible. We had talked about that—how you can't have one without the other. I had come to believe he was committed to making Rock Hill General the best hospital in the area, and that he understood it didn't start in the business office.

He also understood that my job was to see that the patients who came through the ER got the best care possible and that the staff was taken care of. So far, that had never been a source of conflict for the two of us. So far.

Bill was aware of the situation with Amy Connors, and I explained my position. He listened patiently, not saying anything, and occasionally nodded his head in seeming agreement.

Finally, I said, "Bill, we need to do something here. *You* need to do something here. Amy Connors doesn't have anything to do with this—I'm sure of it. She's a solid woman and the best secretary you've got. I don't know why Walter Stevens has personally convicted her, but he's dead wrong. She's been singled out for some unknown reason, and she's being harmed. I'm asking you to step in and help her. Tell Stevens to back off, and if he needs more time to investigate…well, what's the sudden rush?"

Chalmers sat quietly, studying the back of his hands.

"Robert, I hear everything you've said, and I completely understand your position in this matter. But let me explain where I am in this. I've given Walter the assignment of solving this trouble—actually, he asked for it and I agreed—and I have to support him in his findings. If I don't do that, it will undermine his position in this administration and cause irreparable harm. I'm sure that as the director of the ER, you can understand that."

"But what about Amy?" I asked him. "What about the irreparable harm done to her?"

He started rubbing his hands together, and there was a look of concern on his face.

"Robert, I know how close you are to Amy Connors. I hear you, and believe me, I understand what you're having to deal with."

This seemed genuinely painful for him, and I waited as he began stroking his chin.

Finally, he took a deep breath, sighed, and said, "I know how you feel about Walter Stevens. And I know you think he's misguided with the way he's handling this. In fact, I probably feel the same way. But I see a different side of him. He's determined to help make Rock Hill General the best it can be, and I have to admire that."

He paused, then sighed once more.

"I just have to stick with my vice president on this one. My hands are tied, Robert. I'm sorry."

"But Bill—" I tried one more time.

"Robert, I'm sorry. My hands are tied."

There was nothing left to say, and I turned and walked out of the office.

Walter Stevens was standing beside the secretary's desk, pointing out something to her on a report he held in his hand. He looked up as I passed by, and without a word turned his back to me.

Facing the **Darkness**

6:50 p.m. Three days had passed, and we hadn't heard anything from Amy. Virginia had tried to call her in the morning, but there was no answer and her voice mail was full.

"I'll try again tomorrow," she told me when I came in to begin my night shift. "And just so you know, Walter Stevens came down here this afternoon. He wanted to know if any more drugs were missing, and when I told him no, he seemed to take great satisfaction. I told him it had only been three days. Then he looked at me and said, 'Case closed.' It was all I could do to hold my tongue."

Word of Amy's firing had quickly spread through the ER and throughout the hospital. The reason for her firing was known by a growing number of people in the department, and it would be impossible to keep that from spreading as well, try as we might.

"Virginia, it really bothers me that the person who's been stealing the drugs knows that Amy's been fired, and probably knows why. Yet they haven't come forward and are willing to let her take the fall. It's bad enough to be doing this in the first place, but to knowingly allow someone else to suffer for it, and Amy with kids…"

"I know, and it stinks," she huffed. "But what can we do?"

She was right, and I knew it. We were both helpless to do anything for Amy. I wasn't used to that feeling, and I knew it bothered Virginia. I picked up my briefcase and headed to our office.

"Oh, and Dr. Lesslie," she called out to me. I turned and walked back to her. "Darren Adler called in sick again this afternoon. And this

time he *won't* be coming in. Says he can't stop vomiting or some such."
She made this last statement with a measure of skepticism in her voice
and on her face.

"And Patsy Wilson will be coming in. In fact, I think she's already
here, back in the lounge. You'll be working with her and with Clara
Adams tonight."

That will be interesting, I thought, nodding my head.

"Good," I replied, and once more headed down the hallway.

"Well, well—Dr. Lesslie, I presume."

The voice was behind me and was familiar. I turned around and was
facing Patsy Wilson.

"Patsy," I said, leaning forward and giving her a hug. "How long has
it been? Three, four years?"

"How about seven?" she answered.

Ouch! Where had the time gone?

She hadn't changed a bit since she'd last worked in the ER. She had
the same smiling, cheerful face, and the same confident, energetic bearing. It was good to have her back, if only for this night.

"The place looks about the same," she told me, glancing around
the department. "Different faces, but everything seems to be where
it's always been."

"'Don't mess with success.' Isn't that what you always said?" I
quipped.

"Nope. I always said 'If it ain't broke, don't fix it.' So if you're going
to quote me, make sure you get it right."

Clara Adams walked up and asked, "Get what right?"

"Oh, never mind, Clara," I responded. "Have you had a chance to
meet Patsy Wilson?"

"Yes, I have," she answered smiling at the older nurse. "We ran into
each other in the lounge. It turns out we went to the same nursing
school."

"Just a few years apart," Patsy quickly added. "Actually, Clara was
still in diapers when I was in nursing school."

"They had diapers back then?" I teased.

Two charts sat on the countertop, belonging to patients who still needed to be seen. Clara slid one over in front of me.

"Here, why don't you go do something?" she told me with a mischievous smile on her face.

The evening went by smoothly, and it seemed as if Patsy had never left the department. She helped Clara start a difficult IV and later showed her some tricks in effectively delivering a breathing treatment to a wheezing and uncooperative two-year-old.

A little after ten, Jeff Ryan came through triage, pushing a middle-aged man in one of our wheelchairs. I was standing behind the nurses' station and looked up as he passed.

"Cardiac," was all he said, motioning with his head and hurrying toward that room.

Clara had been assigned major trauma and cardiac, and she started off after Jeff.

Patsy was walking out of room 5 and Clara asked, "Patsy, can you give me a hand?"

"Sure, I'll be right there. Let me give these orders to the secretary."

Ozzie Fielder was a fifty-two-year-old man with a long history of diabetes and cigarette smoking. He had come to the ER complaining of chest pain and shortness of breath, and Jeff had immediately noticed his pale color and labored respirations. By the time I got to cardiac, Jeff had him up on our stretcher and was placing electrodes on his bare chest. Next he connected him to our heart monitor.

"Here, let me take over," Patsy said, stepping up beside him.

"Sure," Jeff answered, moving out of her way. He told us what he knew of Mr. Fielder's history and then gave us his vital signs.

"Heart rate is around 50, and his blood pressure's a little over 80. His lungs sound a little wet too."

Ozzie Fielder was having a heart attack and was already getting into trouble. Clara and Patsy were all over him, starting a couple of IVs, getting his oxygen going, setting out the needed medications before I asked for them, and arranging for an expedited trip to the cath lab. Everything went like clockwork, as if these two women had been working together for years. It was great, and I wanted to tell them so.

As Ozzie was being wheeled out of the room by the cath lab techs, I looked at Patsy and Clara and said, "I want the two of you to know you handled that perfectly. It couldn't have gone any more smoothly."

"Hey, we're just doing our jobs," Patsy responded, smiling at her partner. "Isn't that what you always say, Dr. Lesslie?"

"You know what I mean," I mumbled. Patsy knew, and she also knew I didn't give someone a compliment unless I really meant it. "Okay," I groused. "Forget it then. You guys are terrible."

"Now *that's* the Dr. Lesslie we know and love," Patsy chuckled, helping Clara straighten up the room.

The three of us had just walked out of cardiac and over to the nurses' station when we heard a loud commotion from out in triage. It was the voices of several men, angry and cursing, and it seemed to be escalating. Suddenly the ambulance entrance doors opened and Denton Roberts, one of the paramedics on EMS 2, came hurrying into the department. In his arms was a small child, wrapped in a beige blanket that was covered in blood.

"We need major trauma," he called to us, his eyes wide not with fear but with anger.

"Major's open," Clara told him, hurrying ahead and turning on the room's lights.

As he passed me, his head turned toward triage. He heard the yelling and muttered, "How did those guys get here so fast?"

"What are you talking about?" I asked, hurrying along beside him.

With a disgusted look on his face he said, "I'll tell you in a minute, Doc. It's crazy."

Patsy and Clara were standing on each side of the trauma stretcher, ready for Denton and the bundled child.

"Her name is Jenny," he told us, carefully placing her on the thin, sheeted mattress.

Patsy began opening the blanket, a look of growing horror on her face. There was blood everywhere, and when a tiny hand came up toward us with a long gash extending from the wrist to the elbow, Clara gasped.

"It's awful," Denton whispered, staring down at the child, his bloodied hands hanging by his side.

When Jenny had been fully exposed, we just stood there for a split second, looking down in silence and not able to tear our eyes away. I had never seen anything like it. I immediately checked her breath sounds and listened to her heart. For the moment she seemed stable.

I gave Patsy and Clara some instructions and they sprang into action. Then I turned to Denton.

"Tell me what happened."

As he began, the two nurses quietly talked to each other as they gingerly but rapidly undressed Jenny. Clara used the intercom to call for lab and X-ray, and Patsy prepared to start two IVs. All the while, they spoke soothingly to the little girl, and when they could, stroked her tangled and bloody hair, trying to calm and reassure her. She just lay there, strangely quiet, staring up at the ceiling.

"We got a call for a dog bite," Denton said, stepping back from the stretcher and lowering his voice. "Down on Elm Street, about five minutes from here. When we got to the scene, there was a big ruckus out in the front yard, with maybe twenty or thirty people standin' there and hollerin'. We had to push our way through the crowd, trying to find this little girl," he paused, motioning with his head to the stretcher.

Then his face clouded. "It seemed liked no one was worried about Jenny—they were all watchin' two guys fightin' over by this dog pen between these two houses. It was absolute chaos! You know Junior Starr?" he suddenly asked me.

"The guy with all the tattoos on his arms and face?" I responded.

"Yeah, that's Junior," Denton nodded. "He was right in the middle of it with a big hawkbill knife, swingin' it at this other guy, swearin' and sayin' he was gonna kill him."

"Where was Jenny?" I interrupted.

"Like I said, Doc, everybody was watchin' this fight and we had to look around for the 'dog bite.' We saw this woman kneelin' on the ground by the front porch and lookin' down at something. I ran over there and found…It was Jenny's mother, and she was holdin' Jenny in her arms and screamin'. We hadn't been able to hear her with all the other stuff goin' on."

He stopped and looked down at his bloody hands.

"I called Joey over and we got started. She was breathin' and had a good pulse, and she seemed alert. But the whole time, she never made a whimper—she just was lying there, staring up at the sky. I gotta tell ya that it scared me. We both tried to get a line started but couldn't. That's when we called it in and headed to the truck."

He took a deep breath and turned his head to the trauma room door.

"Those guys out in triage, one of them must be Junior Starr," he muttered. "While we were workin' on Jenny we heard someone yell, 'He's been stabbed!' and people started runnin' everywhere. That's about the time the police came down Elm Street with their sirens blarin'. Joey was goin' over to check on those guys but they had already disappeared. I don't know how they did it, but it looks like they beat us here!"

"Who is 'they'?" I asked.

"Junior Starr," he answered. "He owns the pit bull, the one that got loose."

"Pit bull?" I exclaimed, now understanding the damage done to the little girl.

"Yeah, he has a pit bull—Jupiter, they call him. He apparently got loose this evening and went over to Jenny's yard. She was out playin' and didn't see it comin'. No warning or anything. That dog just attacked her and did this…" He again motioned toward the stretcher.

"When her daddy—Toby Ragin—heard the noise, he came out of the house and picked up a shovel and went after the dog. That's when Junior came over, lookin' for Jupiter, and the two got into it. Toby must be out in the waiting room too. He's probably the one who got stabbed."

I had heard enough and stepped over beside the stretcher.

Two lab techs had drawn blood and were hurrying out the door, whispering to each other, while our X-ray tech was preparing to shoot some portable films. Patsy and Clara had done what they could to clean up Jenny, but nothing could lessen the devastation of what I now saw.

She was lying calmly on her back with her arms at her sides. The deep bite on her right forearm was covered with saline-soaked gauze. There were a dozen or so scattered bite marks on her left arm and hand, and on her right thigh.

But it was her face that grabbed my eyes and wouldn't release them. Her right upper eyelid was ripped from the brow through her lashes, and it flopped aimlessly every time she blinked. There was another gash that started in her right nostril and extended down through her upper lip, gaping open and exposing her upper baby teeth.

Jupiter, the pit bull, had meant business. At her jawline, just above her jugular blood vessels, were two deep bites, the lower one exposing the bone of her mandible.

I was hoping that the left side of her face had escaped this terrible damage, but as I gently moved her head to the right, I saw her ear. The top part was missing, and the lobe had been shredded. It was covered in clotted blood and dangling loosely.

Patsy took a deep breath behind me, looking down over my shoulder. "Do you want me to cover as much as I can with wet gauze?" she asked.

"Yeah," I said, shaking my head. "And we'll need to get in touch with whoever's on for plastic surgery." Then I turned to her and whispered, "I just hope they can put her back together."

She turned to the counter and opened a cabinet, reaching for more sterile four-by-fours. The trauma door opened and a policeman walked in. He stepped over to where I stood and looked down at Jenny Ragin.

His hand flew to his mouth and he recoiled, a look of horror and disbelief on his face. "What in the…" he gasped, reaching out for the wall behind him.

Clara immediately helped the young officer to a stool and he sat down.

"Doc, I had no idea…" he mumbled. "I knew it was a dog bite, but…"

"It's bad, Jimmy," I said, recognizing him from other late-night visits to the ER. "But she's going to live."

There was loud shouting in the hallway, just on the other side of the door.

"Where's my daughter?" a man screamed. "Where's Jenny?"

I quickly looked over to the stretcher, knowing the little girl must have heard this outburst. She didn't move a muscle, just kept staring up at the ceiling. Clara was rubbing her head while Patsy began dressing the wounds on her face.

Jimmy jumped up and headed for the door.

"Doc, you're going to be busy the rest of the night," he told me. "Her father and Junior Starr got in a real fight, and they're both messed up pretty good. We'll have a couple of guys here to keep things under control. And you won't be seeing the mother. She's already on her way to jail—busted one of the firemen who responded to the call."

He disappeared out into the hallway just as we heard another voice, more distant, yelling, "I'm gonna kill him! He killed my dog!"

The door closed and I looked over at Patsy Wilson. She looked up at me, and her jaw was set firmly in anger. She shook her head slowly and then looked back down at Jenny.

Clara continued to stroke the little girl's head, and I thought I could hear her quietly singing. There was a troubled look on her face and her lip trembled.

The door opened again, and Clay Norcutt, the plastic surgeon on call, walked into the room.

Two hours later, I had repaired the lacerations on Toby Ragin's right forearm and released him from the department. He was on his way over to the surgical waiting room with a police escort, having been charged with multiple offenses. Because Jenny was down the hall in the OR, the officers were going to give him the chance to wait there and learn of her progress. It would be several hours before he heard anything.

Junior Starr was on his way to jail. He had a fractured rib, a direct result of Toby's shovel being applied to his chest, but no serious injuries. We were all glad to see him leave.

I looked up at the clock—it was 5:15. Almost two more hours to go, and we were exhausted.

Susan Everett was sitting behind the counter while Patsy and I leaned heavily against it, making some notes on the charts in front of us.

"Where's Clara?" I asked, looking around the area. She was nowhere to be seen.

"I don't know," Patsy said, looking up from Junior Starr's ER record. "I haven't seen her in the past half hour or so."

Susan waved her hand to get our attention, and without saying a word pointed over her shoulder to the observation room.

"I'll go check on her," Patsy said quietly, pushing the chart away from her. "This can wait."

She walked over to the door of OBS, looked around for a second, and then disappeared from view.

"What's going on?" I asked Susan.

"Don't know," she answered, not looking up from her work. "I saw her go in there about forty-five minutes ago, but she didn't say anything to me. Looked upset though, and she hasn't come out."

I looked over at the entrance to OBS and wondered what was going on. My better judgment told me to stay where I was.

Half an hour later, Clara walked out of the room and past the nurses' station. I was sitting there with Susan, and the young nurse briefly glanced over at me. Her eyes were red and she tried to muster a smile before disappearing down the hallway.

Patsy Wilson came out of OBS and walked over to where we sat. She took a deep breath and pulled over a chair. As if knowing Patsy and I needed to talk, Susan stood up and said, "I'm going back to the lounge for some coffee. Either of you need anything?"

"I'm fine," I told her.

"Nothing here," Patsy said.

And then we were alone.

"Well," I said slowly. "What was that all about? Is Clara okay?"

"She's *going* to be okay," Patsy said with a tone of both concern and resolve. "Clara's not as tough and hardened as we are. She apparently has seen a lot of difficult stuff recently, and her emotions have been building up. They have a way of doing that down here, you know."

She glanced over at me and I silently nodded in agreement.

"And then all this tonight with Jenny—that was just too much for her to handle. What she needs is to be able to talk with someone who's been there."

Her face clouded over and she didn't say anything. Then she took a deep breath and looked up at me.

"She really likes it here, and she really likes the staff—even *you*," she poked at me. "But you know, we all need someone to lean on from time to time—a sort of mentor, I suppose."

"You mean like Virginia was for you?" I said, smiling at her.

"Like Virginia has been for a *lot* of nurses." She nodded her head. "And for a few hardheaded doctors," she added, raising her eyebrows and looking squarely at me.

"Clara's going to make a great ER nurse," Patsy continued, her tone leaving no room for doubt. "And you're not going to lose her. I'm going to talk with Virginia and see if someone, maybe Lori Davidson, can take her under their wing for a while. I think that's all she's going to need. It's just that we all have our breaking points. There will come a time when…when we…"

She couldn't go on and turned her face from me. I thought I knew what she was thinking—about her *own* breaking point that day in the ER. And I gave her some time.

We both sat in silence, until finally I asked, "What about *you*, Patsy?"

She looked over at me with a puzzled expression on her face that gradually changed to one of uncomfortable understanding.

"Me?" It really wasn't a question, but a sigh of resignation.

She knew what I was talking about, and there was a growing sense of release in her eyes and voice as she began telling me why she had left the ER seven years ago.

"Stu Lowry and I were close friends. Looking back on it, I can understand how that might have seemed…how you might have wondered what the big deal was when I left the ER. After all, everybody liked Dr. Lowry. I know the two of you were friends."

"Yeah, I still miss him," I told her. "Virginia told me you were friends all through school."

"Virginia doesn't know the whole story."

Patsy took a deep breath and leaned back in her chair.

"Stu and I were *more* than friends in school. We were childhood sweethearts, all the way through college. We were like one person, and we both always took it for granted that we would one day be married. Then Stu applied and was accepted into medical school. His family was really excited about that, but they didn't have the money to help him. He scraped together some small scholarships to make it through the first year. But it was really going to be tight for him, and we both knew it just was the wrong time for us to be getting married. But neither of us would bring it up."

She paused and looked away. When she next spoke, her voice was quiet, almost mournful.

"And then I was pregnant."

She looked into my eyes again, and I just listened.

"I didn't tell Stu. I didn't tell anyone. I was afraid that if he found out, he would insist on getting married right then and…That's what I wanted, but I knew it wasn't right for him. And I started pushing him away.

"That was the hardest thing I have ever done in my life, Dr. Lesslie. And when I look back on it…I know now it was a mistake—a terrible mistake. But that's what I did. Of course he didn't understand. He kept coming to see me and calling and…But I knew what I had to do. Stu was not just smart—there was something special about him. And I knew he would someday be a gifted doctor. I couldn't get in the way of that."

She stopped for a moment, and there were tears in her eyes.

"And then the phone calls stopped. A few weeks later, I lost the baby. He never knew. No one has ever known, not until tonight. But Stu was gone, and my life went on. I tried to make myself believe it had never happened, but that didn't work. I just stayed away from our old friends and never went to any of our high-school reunions. The next time I saw Stu was when we were working here in this hospital. We were both married with children, and we were both happy. It was wonderful to see him then, but it was different, in a way I hadn't expected. Nothing would ever change what we had had all those years ago. But I knew without a doubt that the Lord's hand was in everything that had happened to us. And I absolutely knew I loved my husband and my children and where my life had taken me.

"But that morning when Stu came into the ER and was…Everything seemed to come down on me at once and I needed to get out of here. Now, looking back, I realize I had never really dealt with the heartbreak and pain, and the terrible loss. So I left the ER. I ran away."

She stopped and was silent.

"Did it help?" I asked her quietly. "Leaving the ER?"

"No, leaving the ER didn't," she sighed. "But I took the time to work on things, to face all that had happened. That part helped. But I've missed this place, and I've missed you guys. The ER is where I belong."

Now I understood why Patsy had left. I was humbled and moved that she would share all of this with me. And I knew that the Lord's hand was still at work here. My voice cracked a little as I said, "Patsy, I think we both know who Clara's mentor should be."

She must have heard the emotion in my voice because she quickly looked over at me, searching my face.

"Well, it's five 'til seven," Susan announced, walking up to the counter. "Looks like we're gonna make another twelve-hour shift."

I looked at Patsy, smiled, and stood up.

"You're right, Susan," I told her. "We did."

By the end of that long night, we had an innocent little girl in the operating room, two belligerent men and a woman under police arrest, the fortunate save of a young nurse—Clara Adams—and the return of a lost treasure—Patsy Wilson.

16

A Hard Lesson

6:55 p.m. "Okay, Robert—I'm going to show you I learned my lesson."

It was Liz Kennick, and she had just stepped out of room 5. She was excited about something and motioned for me to follow her to the other side of the nurses' station.

I was her relief tonight and had just walked into the department. The place was busy, with people and charts everywhere.

"Come on over here," she said impatiently. "I need to show you something."

With the clipboard of room 5 in her hand, she walked around the nurses' station to the X-ray view box. I followed, wondering what was going on.

There was an X-ray folder lying on the small table below the box, but no films were hanging. Liz put her hand on the folder, apparently making sure I wouldn't pick it up and open it.

"Now, what was the lesson you taught me the other day?" she asked. "The one you said was so important for every ER doc?"

"Hmm," stroking my chin and feigning intense concentration. "'Don't spit in the wind!' No, wait a minute. It was 'Don't let 'em see you sweat!' That was it."

"Oh, come on!" she exclaimed, a look of exasperation on her face. "You know what I'm talking about. 'Don't make assumptions!' That's what you told me."

"Did I say that?" I replied with a puzzled look.

She didn't pay any attention and handed me room 5's chart.

"Take a look at that."

It was the record of a three-year-old boy with a chief complaint of "abdominal pain." Quickly scanning the chart, I noted that his heart rate was fast at 120 and his temperature was 103.

"Wow, looks like this little chap might be sick," I said, giving her back the clipboard. "What's he got?"

"Well, this is very interesting," she began, her face animated and her voice energized. "About an hour ago, the mother of the boy in room 5—his name is Chip Flanders—told me they had been down at the beach visiting some relatives. Chip had gotten hold of a magnet and swallowed it. Of course they all panicked and went to an ER down there. They had X-rays made," she paused briefly, patting her hand on the radiology folder, "and the ER doctor told her Chip would be fine. The magnet was not too big and was rounded on both ends. It had passed through his stomach and was in the small intestine. He said it should move on through in a few days and not cause any problems. Since they were going to be home in a day or so, the doctor there told them to follow up with their pediatrician here in Rock Hill."

That sounds reasonable to me, I thought. There was nothing unusual in what she was telling me. I reached down for the X-ray folder but Liz slammed her hand down again.

"Not so fast!" she corrected me. "You haven't heard the rest of it."

I stood back a little and teased her. "Is there a point to this story?"

She looked at me, doing her best imitation of Virginia Granger, and said, "Be patient. I'm getting to it."

The she turned back to the view box and continued. "Chip was okay for about a day, but they never saw the magnet. And then he started getting sick. First he complained of some stomach pains, and then he started lying around and not moving much. They thought about going back to the ER but decided to come home and see their doctor. On the ride back, he started vomiting and running a fever, and they came straight here. He's been vomiting what looks like bile, and his belly is rock hard."

"Have you called a surgeon?" I asked her, becoming more concerned. She was describing a surgical abdomen, and it sounded like Chip needed to be in the operating room as quickly as possible.

"Dr. Scott has already been down and is going to take him to the OR as soon as they can get the crew ready," she told me. "We've got two lines going and antibiotics. He's ready to go."

"Well, what does he have?" I asked her, puzzled. "You said the magnet was small and rounded and had made it through his stomach. That shouldn't be the problem. Is it his appendix, and the magnet is a red herring?"

"Nope, it's not his appendix," she answered, picking up the X-ray folder and handing it to me. "And the magnet is not a red herring. Take a look."

I opened the folder and put Chip's X-ray on the view box. It was a "kiddie-gram," one X-ray that showed most of his entire body. His whole chest and abdomen were in view, and right in the middle of his belly was the white outline of the magnet.

Just as Liz had described, it was rounded on both ends and was about the size of a small Tootsie Roll. Actually, it was smaller than that, and should easily pass through the rest of his GI tract. The critical thing was that it had cleared his esophagus and stomach, the narrowest points, and the places where foreign bodies can become lodged and cause problems. And I had seen stranger things passed without any trouble—coins of all sizes, pop-tops from soft-drink cans, paper clips, marbles, and even a drill bit from an electric drill.

I scanned the entire X-ray but didn't see anything unusual. *What was I missing?*

"What do you think?" she asked, with a growing coyness that was starting to bug me. After all, who was the teacher here?

"Well, I think he should pass this magnet without any trouble and that his surgical belly is coming from something else."

"What if I told you that one plus one equals one?" she asked cryptically.

"One plus one...What are you talking about?" I was getting a little frustrated.

"What if I told you that Chip swallowed *two* magnets and not one?"

I looked over again at the view box.

"I would say that he had already passed one on the way to the hospital at the beach," struggling for an explanation for this new twist. "Or that he never swallowed it in the first place." Maybe *that* was the errant assumption, that there were two magnets initially, but now only one. *But if that was the case, where was the other one?*

Liz stepped nearer to the X-ray. "Take a closer look."

I didn't know why, but I found myself leaning in toward the view box just as she had done. I studied the film again, and then focused on the magnet.

"Whoa!" I exclaimed. "Would you look at that!"

"That's something, isn't it?" she said, stepping back a little. "Chip's mother told the ER doc that two magnets were missing, but he said the same thing you did. Either he passed one or never swallowed it in the first place."

"But there it is," I said, pointing to the spot on the X-ray. "Or there they are."

When I had looked closer at the magnet, I thought I saw something unusual. And as I studied it more, I had suddenly realized what I was seeing. It wasn't one magnet, but two. And they were almost perfectly overlapping each other. Almost. If you took the time to look closely, you could see two edges and not one.

So that was it. One plus one *did* equal one. They had become stuck together and wouldn't move on down. But why the surgical abdomen? Had they caused some kind of perforation, or leaked some corrosive chemical?

"Mrs. Flanders and I tried to piece this together," Liz began to explain. "It looks like Chip swallowed these magnets at two different times and they were moving through different parts of the small intes-tine. When they passed near each other, they stuck together, just like... Well, just like magnets. But there was the intestinal wall between them, and over a day or so they rubbed together and wore a hole and stuff started leaking out. And Chip got sick. Really sick."

"Wow, you're right," I quietly uttered. "This is really interesting. I've never heard of anything like this happening. Great job, Liz. I'm glad you took the time to look at this film. The answer was right there all along. You know, you saved this boy's life."

Liz nodded her head and with a playful look in her eyes said, "Just remember, Robert—never make assumptions."

She walked back over to the nurses' station and I was about to follow, when Lori Davidson stepped out of the medicine room and called out to me.

"Dr. Lesslie, have you got a minute?"

The place was crazy, but I knew Lori had worked the day shift and should be gone by now. Something was up, and she needed to talk with me.

I headed for the medicine room and said, "Sure, Lori. What's on your mind?"

She turned around and quickly moved back into the small room. I followed and stood facing her near the window, thankful for the relative quiet of this space.

"It's been a little more than three weeks since Amy left the department," she began. "And Virginia and I have been paying close attention to the narcotics cabinet. Nothing has been missing or tampered with."

I also hadn't heard anything, and had assumed that if something was going on, I would have been told. While that was good news, it made things look worse for Amy Connors.

Lori must have been having the same thought.

"Somebody this morning made a remark about that," she told me. "And they were wondering if Amy in fact had been the one stealing the medicine, since it stopped when she left. I just can't believe people sometimes," she added with growing anger in her voice. "There is no way that Amy was responsible. It's just that whoever *is* responsible must be pretty smart. They're lying low right now, biding their time. Don't you think?"

"No doubt they're smart," I agreed. "And I also think it's just a matter of time. Something's going to give, Lori. This kind of thing just doesn't go away."

I was wondering if this was what she had wanted to tell me. But the troubled look on her face told me there was something else, some other reason for her wanting to talk with me.

"I talked with Amy yesterday," she said, and then fell silent.

When she didn't say anything else, I asked, "How is she? Has she found a job yet?"

"Not yet," Lori answered. "But she's been looking. And Dr. Lesslie," she added, pausing and looking away.

"Yes?" I prompted her.

She looked at me again and said, "She's really hurt by all of this. At first she was angry, with the administration and Stevens and all. But then she started wondering why you and Ms. Granger hadn't done more to help her. She asked me if you two thought she was guilty."

"She what?" I exclaimed, astonished. And then I felt an uncomfortable guilt begin to steal over me. *Had we done enough? Had we left this young woman, a friend, to fend for herself?*

"I know," Lori responded. "I tried to talk with her about that, but she's still upset. It'll take some time, but she'll understand that your hands were tied. There was nothing that either of you could do."

It was what I had suspected and what I had feared. This was an empty, awful feeling, and I just stood there staring out the window into the ER parking lot.

"There *is* something you could do to help her," Lori added. "If you would consider doing it."

Quickly turning to face her, I said, "What? What kind of help does she need?"

"She won't ask you in person," Lori explained, shaking her head. "And please don't try to contact her, not yet anyway. But she's trying to find a job, and she'll need a reference, a recommendation. She wanted to see if you and Ms. Granger would be willing to do it. She won't ask anyone else here at the hospital, and she hasn't worked anywhere else in a long time."

"Of course I will," I told her emphatically. "When does she need something? I'll get it done tonight."

Lori smiled up at me. "She'll be glad to hear that. She was afraid that…" She stopped, obviously trying to choose her words carefully.

"Tell her I didn't hesitate," I said. "And I'll have it ready in the morning. And tell her…you tell her…" I didn't know what to say.

"I'll tell her," Lori said, smiling again, and heading back out into the department.

I stood there by myself in the medicine room for a few moments, wondering how we had gotten to this place.

"Doc, we've got a bad burn in major trauma!"

It was Darren Adler, and he almost knocked me down as I walked back to the nurses' station.

"Dr. Nivens is in there now, and I'm gettin' some morphine," he told me, disappearing into the medicine room.

I could now hear the cries of a young child coming from just down the hall.

"Two-year-old girl," Susan said as I passed her at the nurses' station. "Looked like she was in a lot of pain when they brought her in."

I hurried into major and found Ted Nivens standing beside the stretcher, looking down at a screaming toddler. Lori Davidson was the only other person in the room. He looked up at me as I approached the bed.

"Hot-water burns," he said quietly. "Second degree, maybe even some third."

The little girl looked up at me with wide, terrified eyes, and continued to scream. Every once in a while we could understand "Momma!" but the rest was unintelligible.

The left side of her body, from the neck down to her knee, was nothing but angry blisters and raw flesh. Miraculously, her face had been spared. But the burns covered at least 30 percent of her body, making this a very serious and possibly life-threatening injury.

I turned to Ted and asked, "How did this—"

"I'll tell you how it happened!" Darren interrupted. He had just come back into the room and was standing right behind me.

"Here, Lori," he said, handing her an opened vial of morphine. "I cracked the top off and it's ready to go."

She had just finished starting an IV and was going to push some of the pain medicine directly into the little girl's vein.

"Her mother's drunk and wasn't payin' any attention," he explained, anger rising in his voice. He stepped around me and moved closer to the stretcher. "Cindy here was playin' in the kitchen and her mother went outside to smoke a cigarette. She had somethin' boilin' on the stove and Cindy reached up and pulled it over on herself. I don't know how in the world it missed her face, but the rest of her…"

He couldn't say anything else and all of us stood there, looking down at Cindy, and knowing the terrible journey she had just begun. Her skin was peeling off in sheets, and what wasn't peeling was forming gigantic fluid-filled blisters. She would spend the next few weeks in a burn center, undergoing multiple, painful skin grafts, and hopefully surviving. Then she would spend the rest of her life dealing with the scars.

"She doesn't deserve this," Darren muttered. "Her mother ought to be…"

I took him by the shoulder, gently turned him away from the stretcher, and led him toward the door.

"That's not going to do Cindy any good," I told him.

"I know, Doc," he mumbled, looking down at the floor. "But I've got a little boy her age, and I can't imagine him goin' through somethin' like this, and me knowin' that it didn't need to happen. She didn't ask for this. It's her mother. I talked with her out in triage and she's dead drunk! She can barely stand up!" His face was beet-red, and I could understand why. But I had meant it when I said it wasn't doing Cindy any good. And it wasn't doing Darren any good either.

"Come on out to the nurses' station," I told him, pushing the door open and guiding him in that direction. "You can help Susan get in touch with the burn center in Augusta. We need to get Cindy down there as quickly as we can. And why don't you call DSS. They need to know about this."

Darren went straight to the counter and picked up one of the phones. I heard him ask Susan for our directory, and I was glad he had something to do now. Maybe this would give him a chance to cool off.

"Anything I can do?" I asked Ted. Cindy was quieter now, feeling the effects of the morphine. She had two IVs going, and Lori had placed an oxygen mask on her face.

"We'll need to talk with her mother and let her know what's going on," Ted answered. "Then we need to get in touch with the burn center."

"Darren's working on that now," I told him. "Why don't you stay in here, and I'll go find Cindy's mother. Or hopefully someone sober enough for me to talk to."

"That would be great, Robert," Ted said. "I'm not sure I want to deal with any of the family just yet. I'm sorta feeling like Darren right now."

I understood what he was saying, and the anger they were both feeling. I had been there before, a lot of times. But I had seen anger turn excellent ER doctors and nurses into cynical, burned-out, and ineffective people. I struggled not to follow that path.

Sometimes it was harder than others, like the night I saw Missy Jones.

February 1978. 11:45 p.m. I was working in the ER in Greenville and it was the dead of winter. The forecasters were predicting a heavy snowstorm in another day or two and that news must have kept people at home and in bed. We were strangely quiet, and I was sitting in the nursing area with some of the staff and one of the police officers who provided security for the emergency department.

"Doc, have you guys seen any of the 'Red Devil specials'?" the officer asked me.

I wasn't sure what he was talking about and was about to ask, when one of the nurses said, "We had one the other night."

"Yeah, and two last week," another nurse joined in.

"What are you talking about?" I asked, confused.

"Well, Doc," the officer began, leaning forward in his chair. "We started seeing a lot of this a month or so ago. I guess the word got out that it was an effective means of self-protection, and a bunch of people—mainly women—started using it. They buy a bottle of Red Devil lye and pour it into a Mason jar and keep it by their bedside at night. If someone breaks into the house, they throw that stuff right in the face of the guy. Works better than a gun, and it's a lot cheaper."

"You're kidding!" I exclaimed, imagining the damage caused by this caustic chemical.

"The one we had a few nights ago had to go to the OR," the nurse explained. "He must have swallowed some, and it burned his mouth and esophagus. They're not sure he's going to live."

"The other two were burns of the face and neck," the other nurse added. "They weren't life-threatening, but that stuff causes some bad damage."

I had been off for a couple of days and hadn't heard anything about this.

"We're trying to put a stop to it," the officer told us. "But the stuff is easy to buy, and we've been seeing a lot of break-ins lately for some reason. People are scared. I'm sure it's just a matter of time before you see your first one," he added, looking over at me.

To this day, I don't know how he knew, but the door leading out to the triage area burst open and the triage nurse ran into the department carrying a young child in her arms.

"Dr. Lesslie! Get over here quick!" she called out to me, heading to the nearest empty room and carefully putting the child down on the stretcher.

We all jumped up from our chairs and headed over to the screaming little girl. The police officer darted toward the triage entrance, his hand on the butt of his firearm. We had heard loud yells, and there was no telling what was going on outside those doors.

"What happened?" I asked the triage nurse, looking down at the girl. She was clawing at her face and eyes and her horrifying cries were becoming garbled. Foam was coming out of her mouth, and she started gurgling.

"Her name's Missy—Missy Jones," the nurse said breathlessly. "And it's lye burns!"

"Lye burns?" I echoed, not believing what I was hearing.

"Red Devil lye!" the nurse clarified.

We sprang into action—one nurse starting an IV, another restraining Missy's flailing arms while another was suctioning the ever-increasing foam from the little girl's mouth and throat. One of the techs was getting the supplies together to start irrigating her face, eyes, and upper body.

I was preparing to secure her airway and turned to the triage nurse.

"Do we know what happened?"

"I couldn't get much from the mother," she began to explain, catching her breath and calming down a little. "But the boyfriend told me she keeps a glass of Red Devil lye on her bedside table, and Missy came in while the mother was asleep and must have pulled it over on herself."

"That's not the way it happened," the police officer said, walking into the treatment bay. "When Missy walked into the bedroom, it startled her mother, and without thinking she threw the lye in her girl's face."

One of the nurses gasped.

My heart sank as I looked down on Missy's destroyed face. The cornea of one eye was completely clouded over, gone. And the other was bright red and steamy. The skin of her left eyelid and the left side of her face had disappeared, eaten away by the lye.

As I passed an endotracheal tube through Missy's throat, I was shocked by the amount of swelling and damage I was seeing. Her mouth and pharynx were puffy and red, and her vocal cords were already swelling and purple. I was lucky to get the tube through and in place.

"Doc," the officer said, standing right behind me. "The mother wants to come back."

Suddenly it seemed that every eye in the room was on me.

My face was flushed and I was trembling with anger. I wasn't sure Missy was going to survive this, and even if she did…

"No!" I said, my voice tight, and as controlled as I could make it. "Not yet."

I knew the anger I was feeling was doing me no good, and it wasn't helping Missy.

Somehow I was able to put it behind me—at least for two days. Then Missy died, and I became angry all over again. This time it didn't go away.

One day Virginia Granger called me into her office and closed the door behind us. She didn't sit down behind her desk, but took the chair right beside me, pulled it close, and leaned toward me.

"Robert, when I was in the army, stationed overseas, I worked with a surgeon, Major…no, his name doesn't matter. What *does* matter is that he was one of the best trauma surgeons I had ever been around. Great ability and a great attitude. But one day we had three young recruits injured in a training accident. It was a freakish thing, and these boys were really mangled. The problem was that it had been caused by an officer who had been out drinking the night before. That really set off the surgeon, and it was all I could do to keep him calm and focused on the injured soldiers.

"He told me later that his younger brother had been killed by a drunk driver. He apologized and told me he thought he had gotten over it, but it was obvious he hadn't.

"We worked with those boys all day and night, and early in the morning we lost one. The other two were eventually shipped back to the States. But they were never going to be the same. One lost both hands, and the other lost an eye and part of his face. It was awful.

"The surgeon never recovered from that night. He just was never the same. We tried to help, but all we could do was watch as he became more and more angry, and more withdrawn and sullen. Finally he transferred out of there. I don't know what happened to him. In fact, I don't even know if he stayed in medicine."

She was looking at me intently now, studying my face, and for a moment she didn't say anything. I knew what she was telling me and what she was trying to do.

"Here, I want you to have this," she said, handing me a folded slip of paper. "Keep it with you."

She got up and walked out of the office, closing the door behind her. I sat there alone with my thoughts, staring at the paper in my hand. I unfolded it and started reading. The first part had been carefully typed, and it was clear and legible. Underneath those words was something in Virginia's own handwriting, and it took a little longer to make out.

> *Anger is a killing thing; it kills the man who angers,*
> *for each rage leaves him less than he had been before—*
> *it takes something from him.*
>
> —Louis L'Amour

If you don't have something in you that's above you,
you soon give in to the things around you.

I knew she was right, and that Louis L'Amour was right. What I was feeling was killing me and taking something from me. Just like the army surgeon's anger had taken something from him. And I realized my anger was changing me too. I needed to release this to the One above me.

I folded up the paper and slipped it in my pocket. This wouldn't be the last time I would need to read it and be reminded.

Ted Nivens and Lori Davidson were still standing by the stretcher, working with Cindy, who was lying quietly now. I turned and walked out of the room.

I was on my way out to triage to find Cindy's mother, and as I passed the nurses' station Darren looked up at me. His eyes still burned with anger. I recognized myself in those eyes. He needed Virginia's wisdom.

I caught his eyes and said, "Darren, when I get back, let's sit down."

17

Busted

7:35 a.m. In less than a week, it started all over again.

"Dr. Lesslie, can you come here a minute?"

Lori Davidson was standing in the doorway of the medicine room, motioning for me to join her.

When I got there, she was standing in front of the narcotics cabinet, unlocking one of the doors with her keys.

"I need to show you something," she said, reaching into the cabinet and picking up a box of medicine. It was the same type of container Walter Stevens had shown me a few weeks earlier. This time, I knew exactly where to look.

"Hmm," I murmured, stunned at this development. "More Demerol."

I counted six tiny perforations in the bottom of the box, neatly spaced for proper balance, just like before.

"Do you have any idea when this might have happened?" I asked Lori, putting the box of Demerol down on the counter and reaching into the cabinet for another. My mind was racing and I was trying to get a handle on this.

"That's the only one," she told me. "I checked twice. But look at this."

She reached to another shelf and picked up an open box of morphine vials. Before she handed it to me, she pointed down to the narcotics logbook on the countertop. Then with her index finger, she moved down to today's date and the morphine column. The number "9" had been written in the small space, indicating there should be nine vials of morphine in the open box.

I glanced at the container in her hand and counted nine. *That matched. So what was the problem?*

Lori moved her finger over just a little, to the place where the counting nurse puts their initials. *D.A.*

"Okay?" I asked, puzzled. At least this part seemed to be in order.

"Now look at this," she said, handing me the box of morphine.

Once again, I counted nine vials, all unopened and all intact. Then
I withdrew one of the vials and rolled it around between my thumb
and index finger.

"What! How did this happen?"

The vial in my hand was Vistaril, not morphine. Someone had
intentionally switched it out and pocketed the narcotic.

"I just noticed it a little while ago," Lori explained. "I don't know
what made me do that, but I took a couple of them out and saw they
had been changed. From the top, they all look the same."

"How many…?" It didn't matter. My mind was reeling and a hundred thoughts were screaming for my attention. But almost immediately, I latched onto one pressing realization.

"Amy!" I exclaimed. "This will clear Amy! Whoever's been doing
this has finally tipped their hand, and it can't be her!"

I'll get Virginia, and we'll go to Bill Chalmers and set this straight!

I must have been turning toward the doorway because Lori stopped
me.

"Hold on, Dr. Lesslie," she said patiently. "There're some things we
need to think about."

I turned to face her and then glanced over again to the narcotics
cabinet.

"No, that's all that's been tampered with," she said, following my
gaze. "But we need to be careful about a couple of things. I've already
talked with Ms. Granger and told her about this. She had to go to a
mandatory management meeting this morning and won't be back 'til
around noon. And she asked me to tell you about this, but to be sure
you didn't do anything—not until you two can talk."

She was looking up at me, and seemed to be waiting to be sure I
was listening.

I had heard what she'd said, but my brain was in overdrive. We
needed to get in touch with Amy, and there was the matter of the

switched medicines. You can give morphine intravenously without any problems, but IV Vistaril will burn a person's veins and can cause other problems. *If an unknowing nurse reached into the morphine box and took out a vial of Vistaril...*

As if Lori was reading my mind, she said, "I've been off for two days and just noticed this a little while ago. But I checked, and we haven't given much morphine over the past forty-eight hours, so I don't think anyone has been given the wrong medicine. No one has said anything, and that's something that would stand out, don't you think?"

"It should," I mused, considering other possibilities. If the person who had switched the two drugs was also the person dispensing them, it would be a simple matter to disguise their actions. But that person—almost certainly a nurse—wouldn't always be working. And that left open the possibility of one of our patients being given the wrong medicine by mistake. That would be a disaster, and I felt my face flush with anger as I thought about it.

"Here," I said to Lori, handing her the medicine box. "We need to put this somewhere safe, where no one can get their hands on it."

She took it from me and said, "I've already thought about that, and I'm going to take it to Ms. Granger's office."

I looked down again at the narcotics logbook and studied the last entry.

"D.A.," I said softly.

"I know," Lori whispered, a note of sadness in her voice. "I don't want to think Darren could be doing this, but..."

Her voice trailed off. She was coming to the same conclusion I was now being forced to face. I had supported Darren Adler through all of his troubles and had championed his return to the ER. I thought I knew him, and I would never have thought he was capable of stealing and abusing narcotics. But he *had* become a little unpredictable lately, with more and more frequent outbursts of anger. And there had been that little girl the other night with the burns...

"What did Ms. Granger have to say?" I asked Lori, needing to put those thoughts away, at least for a while.

"She had the same response you did," Lori said, nodding her head.

"Her first reaction was to clear Amy's name, but then she started considering other things. She still doesn't know who is doing this, and she doesn't want to do anything to jeopardize catching them. But she *had* to go to that meeting, and she said she wasn't going to talk with anyone until she had a chance to talk with you."

"Okay," I sighed, closing the logbook and looking out into the department. "I guess we'll have to wait. That's hard for me to do. I want to handle this thing head-on and get it over with. But Virginia's right. I need to hear what she has to say. And it looks like we have work to do."

I was almost at the nurses' station when I heard it. Stopping cold in my tracks, I cocked my head toward the hallway and listened.

"Yep, you heard it," Susan Everett said, looking up from behind the counter.

Then there it was again.

Woof! Woof! Woof! It was high-pitched and definitely of canine origin.

"It's a dog, and he's in ENT," she informed me matter-of-factly. "Or she. I couldn't tell which."

"What's a dog doing in the ER?" I asked her, looking down at the clipboard in front of me. *Elva Wilson—69 yr old F.* It was the clipboard for the patient in ENT, and the chief complaint written at the top of the paper was "Nerves tore up."

"You'll have to figure that one out," she chuckled.

I picked up the chart and headed down the hallway.

My hand was on the doorknob, when the dog started barking again. Actually it was more of a yelp or a yip, not really much of a bark. *It must be something small,* I thought.

Stepping into the room, I was assaulted by the odor of mothballs and garlic. Sitting on the stretcher was Elva Wilson, and in her lap was a King Charles spaniel, its eyes now focused unflinchingly on me.

"Ms. Wilson, I'm Dr. Lesslie," I told her, closing the door behind me.

Elva was...well, she was unusual. Her hair was died a bright orange-red, and her ruby-red lipstick had been applied with less than consummate skill. It was smeared onto her cheeks and chin, though she didn't seem to mind or even know. Mascara had streaked down her face, and she was only making it worse by dabbing the tears from her eyes. She wore a navy-blue housecoat and bright pink slippers.

"Hello, Dr. Lesslie," she sobbed out. "I'm Elva Wilson, and this is Princess," she added, looking down at her pup. Her accent was heavy, eastern European—maybe Hungarian.

On cue, the tiny dog wagged her tail and yipped at me.

"Ahem!"

Startled, I turned around to see an elderly man standing in the corner of the room. I hadn't noticed him when I came in, and until now he hadn't made a sound.

"This is my husband, Barney," she introduced us.

The man took an Atlanta Braves baseball cap from the top of his head, crumpled it in his hands, and bowed slightly to me. His attire was eclectic—a multicolored paisley shirt, pants that were checkered light blue and dark blue, and much-worn leather sandals over white socks.

"Mr. Wilson," I said, bowing in turn. "Nice to meet you."

Elva let out a loud wail and began drying her eyes again. Princess looked up at her, confused and upset. Not able to think of anything better to do, she looked back at me and started yelping.

I looked down at the chart and again read "Nerves tore up." *Where should I start?*

"Dr. Lesslie, you need to do something for Elva." Barney spoke clearly, with no accent and with obvious concern for his wife. He stood there, wringing his cap in his hands and looking at me with pleading in his eyes.

"Tell me what's going on," I asked.

Elva let out another wail, and this time Princess looked up at the ceiling and howled.

"You need to x-ray the dog," he said, and then just stared at me.

"The dog," I said, trying as hard as I could to appear serious. "Why do we need to x-ray Princess?"

"Oohhh!" Elva moaned. This time I didn't turn to her, but kept looking at her husband.

"Yes, you need to x-ray the dog," he began to explain. "A little while ago, Princess ate one of Elva's rings, her favorite, the diamond that her grandmother gave her."

"Aaahh! Grand Ma-ma!" Elva cried.

"She what?" I asked, wanting to be sure I had heard him correctly.

"The dog ate her ring and she is terribly upset, as you can see!" Barney answered, glancing over at his wife. "If we don't get that ring, I don't know what will happen!" he added, nodding at her.

"Oh, my ring!" Elva wailed, clutching Princess to her chest and rocking back and forth.

"Did you think about taking Princess to a vet?" I asked, struggling for some plan here.

"Elva won't have anything to do with that," he answered, shaking his head and looking down at the floor. "She demanded that I bring her here and have the dog x-rayed. What could I do?" he asked, shrugging his shoulders, clearly helpless to disagree with his wife.

"Well, Mr. Wilson, we don't routinely x-ray animals here in the ER," I explained.

"Ooohhh! What will I do? Grand Ma-ma!"

So there we were—Elva was wailing, Princess was howling, and Barney continued to plead with me.

"You see, Doctor? What am I going to do?"

Then I did what any prudent ER doctor would do.

"Mr. Wilson," I told him. "Try to calm your wife down, and I'll be back in just a few minutes."

I escaped into the hallway and quickly closed the door behind me. I could still hear Princess as I hurried back up the hall to the nurses' station.

Jeff Ryan was standing there. He was the triage nurse this morning and had taken the Wilsons back to ENT.

He was writing on a chart and without looking up said, "Doc, there's a depressed cat in room 2, a horse with bronchitis in 5, and a strung-out orangutan in Ms. Granger's office."

I wasn't amused.

"What were you thinking?" I scolded him. "Why didn't you send them to one of the vets in town?"

"You saw Elva," he answered, teasing me. "Her nerves are 'tore up.' What was I supposed to do? She needs some help."

"That's for sure," I agreed, shaking my head. "But what am I supposed to do? Send them around to X-ray for a 'doggie view'?"

"How about a 'small doggie view'?" Susan quipped, not looking up at us.

I glanced down at her and frowned.

"Well, Doc, we've x-rayed stranger things," he said, stroking his chin knowingly.

"What do you mean?" I asked.

"There was that guy a couple of years ago who was sure his two-year-old had swallowed his car key. He was stuck with no transportation and was desperate. We x-rayed the little guy then, remember?"

"I remember," I said. "And right after we did, this father found the key in his back pocket. Now how does that relate to the Wilsons?"

"Well, remember when we had the Halloween candy scare and had all those parents bringing their kids' candy in to be x-rayed? Somebody had heard on the news that people were putting razor blades in candy bars. How many bags of candy did we x-ray?"

For two or three Halloweens we'd had people lined out the door, waiting to have their children's candy x-rayed. The hospital even had to call in extra staff. Finally they refused to do it anymore, and it stopped.

"You're right. I do remember that," I said, beginning to wonder if there might be some precedent for x-raying Princess. After all, it didn't seem we were going to be able to help Elva until we determined whether or not that ring was in her dog's gut.

"And I seem to remember that *someone* on duty that night managed to confiscate a fair amount of Milk Duds," Jeff said, cutting his eyes at me accusingly.

"I don't know who you're talking about," I said innocently. Milk Duds were my favorite candy…it was all coming back to me now.

"And what about Jeremy Fowler?" he asked, again nodding his head.

"Jeremy Fowler." I said the name slowly, unable to keep from smiling.

Halloween, 1986. 9:45 p.m. The back hallway was lined with ghoulies and ghosties and all manner of strange and frightening creatures. Scattered amongst them were a few princesses and pirates, and at least a half dozen Elvis Presleys. They were all impatiently waiting to have their candy x-rayed so they could go home and begin devouring the sugar-laden treats. At one point, I glanced back there and saw an Elvis sneak some bubble gum out of his bag and into his mouth.

As I stepped out of room 5, having examined a patient with a non-Halloween case of possible appendicitis, I almost ran into Jeff Ryan and the man he was leading back to minor trauma. Actually it was a scarecrow, or a very good imitation of one. It was a middle-aged man, looking for all the world like Ray Bolger in *The Wizard of Oz*. Only *this* scarecrow was gingerly holding a bloody rag to his forehead. He managed a smile as he passed me in the hallway.

Jeff had glanced over and grinned at me, nodding his head. When he came back up to the nurses' station a few minutes later, he put the chart of minor trauma B down and said, "Where's Dorothy when you need her? This scarecrow really *does* need a brain."

"What are you talking about?" I asked, intrigued by what I had seen and now just heard.

"Just wait," Jeff replied cryptically. "You know who that is, don't you?"

"Sure," I said, not looking over at him. "A scarecrow."

"No, I mean who that guy *really* is. "

"I couldn't tell," I answered truthfully. "Am I supposed to know him?"

"That's Jeremy Fowler, chairman of the county council," Jeff explained. "You'll recognize him when you get a good look."

I slid the chart of room 5 over to the secretary.

"We'll need a CBC and a urine," I told her. "And don't let him eat or drink anything."

Then I picked up Fowler's chart. *46 yr old M—laceration of forehead.*

"Come on," I said to Jeff. "What's going on here?"

"Just wait," he repeated. "He'll tell you."

Then he disappeared back into the triage room.

I had met Jeremy Fowler on a couple of occasions, and I remembered him as being a nice guy. He had been on the county council when we moved to Rock Hill, and now was the chairman. I wondered how he had lacerated his forehead, and on Halloween.

There were two other patients in minor trauma, both resting quietly and hidden from view behind their drawn curtains. I walked over to bed B, pulled its curtain aside, and stepped over to the stretcher.

"Jeremy," I greeted him. "I'm Robert Lesslie. What happened to you tonight?"

"I'm glad you're on duty tonight, Robert," he said, extending his hand to me. His handshake was firm and strong, and he said, "It seems that I've had a little...mishap."

He took the kitchen rag from his forehead, exposing a three-inch laceration that extended from his hairline down to just above the bridge of his nose.

"Wow," I said softly. "That's a pretty good cut. How did it happen?" I moved closer to him, gently examining the gaping wound and looking for any other signs of trauma.

"Well, I feel sort of foolish..." He stopped and peered around the edges of the curtain, as if making sure no one else could hear him. Then in a hushed voice he told me his story.

"I decided, since it's Halloween and all, that I would do something different this year. We have a lot of kids in our neighborhood and I thought it might be fun if I put a little fear of the Lord in 'em. I dressed up as a scarecrow—wait, you can see that. Looks pretty good, doesn't it?"

He held his arms out and cocked his head to one side. Actually, he had done a great job. There was straw stuffing coming out of the collar of his shirt and his sleeves. And his overalls were loose and well-worn.

"Good job!" I congratulated him, smiling.

"My wife helped me with most of this," he said, looking down at his garb. "She didn't like the idea of what I was going to do, but she helped anyway. She's out in the waiting room and is pretty upset with me."

He glanced around the room again and resumed in a hushed voice.

"Anyway, I got some bales of hay and put them on the porch by the front door, and got a couple of pumpkins and scattered them around.

Then I sat down on one of the bales, leaned back, and got real still. I didn't move a muscle. And pretty soon, the kids starting coming up the walkway. I could hear them whispering, and I'd peek a little and see them pointing at me. But I wouldn't move at all, not until they got right up to the door. And then when they'd ring the doorbell, I'd jump up and holler and wave my arms in the air! And those kids would take off running— screaming and hollering and not looking back. I felt kind of bad—one of the kids' candy bags flew up in the air and landed in the bushes. I hope they've gone back to get it," he added, shaking his head a little.

He was about to go on, when we heard some giggling from the bed next to us. Someone was listening and enjoying this story.

Jeremy looked up and motioned for me to move closer. Then in barely a whisper, he continued.

"That went on for about an hour, and every single trick-or-treater got the willies scared out of them. Every single one. It was great! And I was having a blast."

He paused and his brow, bloodied as it was, furrowed a little.

"Then the little redheaded Bates boy came up the steps. He's about eight, and he was all by himself, dressed up like one of those Star Wars characters. Just like all the other times, I waited and didn't move a mus-cle. He was more cautious than any of the others, and was studying me pretty hard. Never took his eyes off me, and kept a good distance, circling around the porch until he could reach the doorbell. When he rang it, I jumped up and hollered and started waving my arms and all. He took a few steps and then saw the pitchfork I had leaned against one of the bales of hay. That kid's strong for his age, and quick. He dropped his bag of candy, grabbed the pitchfork, and whacked me on the forehead! Knocked me down! Then he grabbed his candy and took off. Never looked back, just kept running."

Jeremy gently dabbed away the small trickle of blood running down his nose.

"Can't blame the boy," he said, smiling a little. "I probably would have done the same thing. Anyway, that's the story, and here I am."

After I finished examining him, we sent the scarecrow around to radiology with the order—*Skull films—whacked by Darth Vader.*

It took a while, but I was able to put our scarecrow back together. I couldn't help him with a new brain, though. He would just have to learn to use the one he had.

I was still thinking about Jeremy Fowler and must have been smiling when Susan repeated herself. "Dr. Lesslie!"

This time she was louder, and she snapped her fingers, trying to get me to refocus.

"Whatever you're thinking about, I don't know if I want to hear it," she told me. "But what are you goin' to do with the woman in ENT?"

I glanced down again at Elva Wilson's chart and made up my mind. Sometimes you just don't need to go by the book. I looked back up at Jeff and said, "We're going to x-ray that pooch."

With a broad smile on his face he turned to Susan and said, "We need a doggie-gram in ENT, stat!"

With a Little Help from My Friends

12:45 p.m. It turned out that Princess had indeed ingested Grand Ma-ma's diamond ring, and I informed Elva and Barney that they would have to wait a day or two to retrieve it. Elva seemed happy with that plan, but Princess seemed a little disconcerted when she heard talk of Milk of Magnesia and castor oil. I would leave that part up to them.

I was standing at the nurses' station when Virginia Granger appeared in the doorway of her office, motioning for me to join her there. I had just finished treating a child in room 3 with an ear infection and was tossing his chart in the discharge basket.

"I'll be in Ms. Granger's office," I told Susan. "If you need me, just holler." I walked around the nurses' station and passed the door of the medicine room just as Lori was coming out.

"Lori," Virginia called to her, still standing in the doorway. "I need you in here for a few minutes."

The two of us walked into her office, and I closed the door behind us. Virginia was already sitting behind her desk, and without a word she pointed to the two chairs in front of her. We obediently followed her silent instructions and took our seats.

"Now *that* was a lot of fun," Virginia said, shuffling some papers on her desk. "Three hours in a management meeting. It's like having your fingernails pulled out one at a time." She sighed and added, "I guess it's important, but we could have handled the significant stuff in about fifteen minutes. Oh well." She pushed the papers to the side of her desk and looked up at us.

"So, Dr. Lesslie, I assume Lori has told you about what she discovered this morning in the medicine room."

"She did, and I—"

She raised her hand, interrupting me. I knew better than to continue, and I waited, knowing she had a plan, and knowing she would unfold it when she was ready. Lori and I looked at each other and then back at Virginia.

She reached across her desk and pulled her telephone over in front of her. Then she dialed some numbers, pushed the speakerphone function button, and hung up the receiver.

We sat there, all of us silently looking at each other, while the phone began to ring. Virginia adjusted her glasses, then peered at me over the top of their heavy black rims. *What is going on?* I wondered.

"Hello."

It was Amy Connors. My head jerked over toward Lori, whose mouth was now hanging open. She was staring down at the phone.

"Hello," Amy repeated.

I looked over at Virginia for some understanding. Still looking over her glasses, she raised her hand and with a ramrod-straight index finger pointed directly at me.

Out of the corner of my eye I could see Lori's head turning toward me.

I was afraid Amy might hang up so I quickly said, "Amy, this is Dr. Lesslie."

There was silence on the other end, and I sat there, waiting.

Finally I repeated myself. "Amy, this is Dr. Lesslie."

"I heard you." The voice was quiet, subdued—and my heart sank a little. "What is it, Dr. Lesslie?"

I looked over again at Virginia, seeking some kind of guidance here. *What could I tell her? How much should I share?*

Virginia nodded her head, and I thought I saw a flicker of a smile at the corners of her mouth.

"Amy, I'm in Ms. Granger's office with Lori, and the three of us are on speakerphone."

Silence again.

"Amy?" I spoke.

"I'm here," she answered, still quiet and restrained. "What do you want?"

I took a deep breath and began telling her about what Lori had found this morning. She didn't say a word as I explained how more narcotics were being stolen, and that the problem was continuing.

"It's what we've known all along," I told her. "You couldn't have had anything to do with this. And pretty soon it will be obvious to everyone else. The administration has made a big mistake and we're going to be sure they make this right."

"And just how are you going to do that?" she asked, with an edge of sarcasm in her voice. "I've been fired, remember?"

"That was a mistake," I persisted. "We all knew that, and we're sorry that happened. *I'm* sorry that it happened. It never should—"

"Amy, this is Virginia Granger," the head nurse interjected, moving the phone closer to her and nodding at me. I gladly let her take over.

"This has all been a terrible mistake, and handled very poorly," Virginia continued. "No one in this department has ever doubted your innocence, and I hope you know that. Our hands were tied once the administration made their decision. But now, with this new evidence, we're going back to Mr. Chalmers and clearing this up. We still have to find the person responsible for this, so I'm asking you not to say anything to anybody about what we've talked about. You are the first person, other than the three of us, to know anything about it."

She paused, waiting for some acknowledgment from the other end.

"Amy?" Virginia gently prodded.

"I'm here," she answered. "And I'm not going to say anything." Her voice was still quiet, and I sensed some suspicion in it. Or maybe it was a lingering hurt.

"This is all going to move pretty fast now," Virginia continued. "And it should all be out in the open soon. In the meantime, though, I want you to be thinking about something."

I looked up at our head nurse, my eyes questioning this last statement. *Where was she going with this?*

Virginia met my eyes, but there was no clue there.

"Amy, we want to have you back in the ER," she said.

There was silence again, and I added, "That goes for all of us. I want you to come back too."

Lori leaned over the desk, close to the phone.

"Amy, this is Lori. I miss you, and I love you."

I glanced over at Virginia and this time there was no mistaking it. She was smiling. When she saw me looking at her, smiling myself, she pretended to scowl at me and turned her head away. But there was that smile again.

Then she once more faced the telephone.

"Amy, this is a lot to be giving you, we know. But just take some time and think about it. And know that when this is all over, we want you back here in the ER."

The three of us sat there, staring down at the telephone, waiting.

"Thanks for calling," Amy finally said. "I've got to go now."

And she hung up.

I leaned back in my chair and let out a long sigh.

Lori looked over at Virginia and asked, "Well, what do you think?"

Virginia had taken off her glasses and was cleaning them, intently studying the bifocals.

"Well, it's about what I expected," she began. "At least she didn't hang up right off the bat. She could have done that, and I wouldn't have blamed her. She's been put through a lot, and for us to call her out of the clear blue like that—well, I think she handled it pretty well."

"But do you think she'll ever come back to the ER?" Lori persisted.

Virginia put her glasses back on and looked at her.

"Only time will tell. Only time will tell."

I was about to say something, when Virginia stood up and said, "Lori, I need to speak with Dr. Lesslie for moment. Would you mind?"

She got up, and with a look of relief on her face said, "I've got plenty to do." As she stepped toward the door she turned and faced her head nurse.

"Ms. Granger, thanks for letting me be here for that." Then she turned and headed out into the department, closing the door behind her.

"We're lucky to have her," Virginia said. "She's a good nurse, and a good woman."

Then she settled back down in her chair and started drumming her fingers on the desktop.

"Now, what are we going to do?" she asked thoughtfully. I knew she wasn't expecting an answer, so I just waited for her to collect her thoughts.

"At some point, we need to let the administration know about this," she mused. "Probably sooner rather than later. But considering how they've handled this so far, I would rather it be later."

"Did you get a chance to look at the narcotics log?" I asked her.

"No, but Lori told me Darren was the last to sign the morphine count. I know how you feel about him, but it's time we sit him down and have a talk. I would rather resolve this without getting Stevens involved again, if we can."

"Are you convinced it's Darren?" I asked, thinking I knew her answer.

"Who else could it be?" she asked. There was sincere concern in her voice, and I knew she wanted there to be some alternative. But there didn't seem to be one. Everything seemed to be pointing to Darren Adler. Maybe I had been wrong all along.

When I didn't answer, Virginia said, "We need to bring him in this afternoon and confront him with all of this. He's your friend, and you know he needs help. This needs to stop before something really bad happens."

She was right, and I knew it.

"When does he work again?" I asked.

She had already taken a copy of the schedule out of the top drawer of her desk and was studying it.

"He's working the three to eleven shift this evening. Why don't we meet with him as soon as he gets here?"

"Okay," I told her. "If I'm busy, just grab me."

There were a couple of patient charts in the *To Be Seen* rack, and I picked up the first one, room 4.

Kim Carlton—26 yr old F—fever. Good. Maybe this would be straightforward. The triage nurse had recorded her temperature as 99.9, and her blood pressure was normal. I checked her heart rate—it was high at 118. Then I noticed that this was Kim Carlton's third visit in as many days. That was always a red flag. So much for being straightfor-ward. Any time a patient came back to the ER, you had to check things a little deeper, pay a little more attention, and look for something seri-ous going on. A third return visit just compounded all of that.

I glanced over the two previous charts. Both times she had come in with a complaint of fever, both times nothing had turned up, and both times she had been sent home. Liz Kennick had seen her initially, and Ted Nivens had seen her just last night. I would be surprised if they had missed something significant.

Kim Carlton was waiting for me in room 4, sitting comfortably on the stretcher. Her husband, Elliott, was sitting on a stool in the corner of the room and got up as I entered.

"Hello, Doctor," he greeted me, shaking my hand. "I'm Elliott Carl-ton and this is my wife, Kim."

"I'm Dr. Lesslie," I introduced myself. "Kim, tell me about this fever you've been having." I leaned back against the counter, while Elliott sat back down on his stool.

"When did it start, and what other symptoms are you having?"

Kim proceeded to tell me her story. She had been doing well up until three weeks ago. She started having some mild headaches and a low-grade fever, and occasional knee and shoulder pains, but nothing else. No cough or vomiting, and no weight loss.

"I've lost my energy," she told me, "and don't seem to be able to do the things I'm used to doing. I tried to run about a week ago and almost collapsed."

"Just so you know, Doc," her husband interjected. "This is a woman who runs half-marathons. So something must be going on."

I nodded my head, impressed by this piece of information, but a lit-tle surprised because of the now-frail appearance of the young woman sitting before me. Elliott was right—something must be going on.

I continued questioning her. After my examination I told the cou-ple we would be checking on some labs and getting a chest X-ray.

"We're going to try to get to the bottom of this today," I told them, determined to do just that.

"Thanks, Dr. Lesslie," Elliott said, getting up and sitting by his wife on the stretcher.

At the nurses' station, I studied the record in front of me and the labs that Liz and Ted had done on her first two visits. Clara Adams had room 4 today, and I asked her to get a urine specimen and draw some blood from Kim.

"They're nice people, aren't they?" she said, picking up some lab slips and making some notations on them.

"Yeah, they are," I agreed, not looking up from the clipboard. "We just need to figure out what's going on with her."

"Now this is odd," I murmured, thumbing through the pages of the record.

"What's odd?" Lori Davidson asked, standing on the other side of the counter.

"Just these labs on the woman in 4," I answered. "Liz got a CBC two days ago, and her hemoglobin was 14. Last night, when Ted checked one, it was 12. That might just be lab variation, but if her hemoglobin is falling, I don't have a clue why. We'll see what today's looks like."

Clara walked back over to where I stood, carrying several vials of blood and a cup of Kim's urine.

"Take a look at this," she said, holding the cup where I could see it.

The urine was dark, almost muddy.

"Did you check it for blood?" I asked her.

"Not yet," she answered. "I thought you would want to see it first."

If that was blood in her urine, it opened up a lot of possibilities. But the fact that it was dark and murky made me wonder if she was breaking down muscle from all of her running. She might be in kidney failure and on the verge of getting into real trouble.

"Nurse!"

Elliott Carlton was standing in the opening of room 4 and calling for help.

"Nurse, can somebody help us?"

Lori immediately headed to their room and disappeared behind the curtain. I finished making some notes on Kim's chart and then quickly followed her.

Kim was sitting on the stretcher, wrapped in a blanket and shivering. But it was more than shivering—she was shaking, and her teeth were chattering. I had never seen anything quite like it, and the contrast between this and her condition just a few minutes ago was startling.

"What's the matter?" I heard Lori ask her.

"I....I...can't get warm," Kim stuttered, her head shaking uncontrollably.

Lori was reaching for another blanket, when Clara walked into the room. She stopped at the foot of the bed and stared wide-eyed at our patient.

"I've seen this before," Clara murmured.

I barely heard what she said, and turned to face her.

"What was that?" I asked, leaning close.

"I've seen this before," she repeated. "My aunt—"

"What about your aunt?" I asked, concerned by her reaction.

Clara didn't answer me, but stepped closer to Kim. "Have you been traveling anywhere?" she asked. "Anywhere out of the country?"

"We just spent our honeymoon in Costa Rica," Elliott answered, stepping up beside the nurse. "It was four or five weeks ago. Why? We were told it was a safe place to travel. And we only drank bottled water."

"It *should* be a safe place," I reassured him, trying to remember some of my travel medicine. "Where did you stay in Costa Rica? What part?"

"We stayed in a place called Quepos, on the Pacific side, and spent a lot of time in the Manuel Antonio National Park. We did some zip-lining and horseback riding. But we didn't get sick while we were there."

Lori draped another blanket around Kim, and her husband jumped up on the stretcher and put his arm around his quivering wife.

"I think that part of Costa Rica is fine," I told him. "As long as you're careful about the water."

Could she have some type of hepatitis or a parasitic infection?

None of this was fitting anything I was familiar with. I turned to Clara and was about to ask her what she was thinking when she asked, "Did you leave the Quepos area? Travel up into the mountains?"

Elliott thought for a moment and then looked up at her with a sudden realization. "We spent two days over near Limón, on the Caribbean side of the country. But we didn't like it much, and we headed back to Quepos. Why? Is that a problem?"

Clara looked up at me and said, "That's it. Kim has malaria, and she's starting to get really sick. Her urine—that's 'blackwater fever.'"

"Malaria?" I exclaimed. "What makes you think she has malaria?"

"What?" Elliott cried, grabbing his wife tightly with both arms. "Did you say malaria? And 'blackwater fever'? What in the world is that?"

"My aunt and uncle were missionaries in eastern Africa," Clara explained. "When they got home, my aunt became very sick, and it took the doctors a while to figure it out. But in the end, she was shaking and looking just like Kim."

"In the end?" Elliott said, looking down at his wife with obvious fear in his voice.

"Not the *end*," Clara said quickly, correcting herself. "She did fine once they made the diagnosis. But it took them a while. Malaria is something that's not very common in the U.S."

"That's for sure," I agreed. "I've never seen a case of it. But what makes you so certain?" I asked the nurse.

"When Mr. Carlton mentioned Limón, I remember reading that there was a fair amount of malaria on the Caribbean side of Costa Rica. Once my aunt was so sick, I wanted to find out as much as I could about the disease and where you could get it. I don't know why that stuck in my mind, but it did."

"But how do we find out for sure?" Elliott asked. "And if it *is* malaria, how do we treat it?"

"We'll find out," I told him. "And we'll treat it."

Then I turned to Lori and said, "Would you get in touch with the lab and tell them I need to speak with one of the pathologists? We're going to be ordering some blood work that's a little out of the ordinary."

Two hours later, we had our diagnosis. Kim did in fact have malaria, and the most serious strain. The hospital's infectious-disease expert was admitting her, and he reassured all of us that she was going to be all right.

"You're going to be in the hospital for a while," he told the couple. "But we've caught this in time, and you're going to be okay."

"Thanks to Clara," Elliott said, smiling at the young nurse.

"Yes, thanks to Clara," I echoed, truly thankful for her help.

She was blushing a little as she left the room and walked over to the nurses' station.

A little after three, Darren Adler walked up the hallway, looking for Lori and for his evening assignment. Before he could find her, Virginia called him into her office and I joined them there.

He was sitting in front of her desk, his hands on his knees, and he nodded as I took the chair beside him.

"What's going on?" he asked both of us. "Am I in some kind of trouble?" He chuckled a little as he said this, then added, "It's not the CCU nurses again, is it?"

I glanced over at Virginia. She wasn't smiling.

"Darren, we need to talk about a couple of things."

Her voice was serious, and her steely glance didn't waver from his face.

He looked over at me, the smile now gone from his face, and his legs started bouncing nervously under the edge of the desk.

"Sure, what is it?" he asked, turning back to Virginia.

"We've had more morphine missing from the narcotics cabinet," she stated bluntly while studying his eyes for a response.

"More missing?" he said, with a surprised look on his face. "I thought that—"

"It wasn't Amy," I interrupted him, knowing where he was going and getting a little angry about it. "It was *never* Amy."

Darren looked at me and then back at Virginia, with the beginning of understanding on his face.

"You don't think…Wait just a minute!" he sputtered angrily. "You don't think *I* have anything to do with this, do you?"

When neither of us said anything he stood up, almost knocking his chair over.

"I'll tell you right now—I don't know anything about those drugs being stolen! Not the Vistaril, or the Demerol, or the morphine! I haven't had anything to do with any of that!" He started angrily pacing the room.

"How did you know about the Vistaril?"

Darren stopped abruptly and turned to Virginia. "How did I…" he stammered, his voice trailing off.

"Only a few of us knew about the Vistaril," she said quietly.

He shook his head, and then with a troubled look on his face said, "I don't know how I knew about that. Maybe Lori said something. I can't remember."

The two stared at each other, locked in a painful contest.

"Look, if you think I'm the one doing this, then just say so," he demanded. "But I'm telling you right now, I don't have anything to do with it. And if you want a drug screen, let's go! I don't have anything to worry about."

My mind flashed back to what Walter Stevens had said all along, that the person stealing these drugs wasn't using them himself, but selling them. If that was the case, any drug screen done would be negative.

"We're going to talk with the administration about that, Darren," Virginia said calmly. "There's a hospital policy concerning any drug testing, and we need to be careful to follow it."

"I don't care about any policy!" he shouted. "I'm ready to be tested right now! This is crazy!"

"We're not going to do that right now," she told him, her voice somehow still calm and professional.

He looked over at me.

"Dr. Lesslie?" His voice was pleading, exasperated.

"Darren," I said. "Your initials were the last ones on the narcotics log right before we found that the morphine was missing. How do you expect us to explain that?"

He looked down, staring at the floor and shaking his head.

"Listen," I continued. "We want to help you with this, but—"

"Help me?" he started to shout again. "Help me? You call this help? I'm telling you, I don't know anything about this! But here's how you can help me—I'm going to work my shift today, 'cause I'm not going to leave you shorthanded, Ms. Granger. But I'm going to take tomorrow off. I need to think about all of this. And if you want to send the police—well, I'll be at home."

Without another word, he turned and walked out of the office, slamming the door behind him.

Virginia and I sat in silence for a few minutes, each of us deep in our own thoughts. I was confused and troubled. *Had I misjudged Darren all along? Or were we still missing something, and if so, what could it possibly be?*

It was Virginia who spoke first. "What was it that Shakespeare said? Something about protesting too much?"

She was looking at me and slowly shaking her head. Suddenly she seemed very tired, and she took off her glasses and began rubbing her eyes.

"What now?" I asked her.

She stared down at her desk for another moment, then put her glasses back on.

"I'm going to sit down in the morning with Bill Chalmers." There was resolve in her voice, but also defeat. "It's time to give this back to him and let him handle it. We tried."

I didn't like that idea, considering how the administration had botched things with Amy Connors. But what else could we do?

"You're right, Ms. Granger. We tried."

I got up and left her alone with her thoughts.

No Explanation Necessary

6:45 a.m. The sun was just beginning to come up as I pulled into the ER parking lot. The dawn of a new day should have cheered me, but my spirit was troubled and a cloud seemed to be hanging over Rock Hill General. There wasn't going to be any good ending to this drug business, and I knew things would never be the same. Our close-knit family had suffered a significant blow, maybe even a fracture…maybe one that couldn't be healed.

Darren Adler had come up to me before I'd left last night and apologized for his outburst earlier. He had even been able to admit that the narcotics logbook looked suspicious. I was glad he had, yet I had the sense he could blow again at any moment.

"You gotta trust me, Dr. Lesslie," he had said. "You gotta know that I don't have anything to do with this."

I didn't know any such thing, but I *wanted* to trust him. I had mumbled something in reply and then left for home.

And now I wondered what *this* day would bring.

I got out of my car and was halfway to the ambulance entrance, when suddenly someone blew their horn at me. Startled, I wheeled around, and there was a brand-new silver truck pulling into a parking space not twenty feet from where I stood.

It's Amy Connors! And she's coming back to work!

I waved and took a few quick steps in that direction. Then I stopped.

One of our OR techs got out of the truck, slammed the door behind her, and said, "Dr. Lesslie, you'd better watch where you're going."

"You're right, Donna, I'd better," I said, trying to hide my disappointment.

"Looks like it's going to be a great day," she added, smiling and hurrying toward the staff entrance.

"Yeah," I muttered, knowing she couldn't hear me. "A great day."

The morning started smoothly enough, with only a handful of routine cases before nine o'clock. I was coming out of room 4 when Virginia walked over, glanced at the empty major trauma room, and motioned for me to follow her.

She flipped on the lights and stepped over to the stretcher. Curious, I followed without saying anything. I wondered if she had talked with Bill Chalmers and something was getting ready to happen.

Virginia looked down at the chart in my hand and said, "Tell me about that man."

Surprised, I glanced down at room 4's clipboard. His name was Jim Barkley and he was seventy-eight years old. He had come in with cough and a fever of 102, and he had a history of a right-sided stroke that left him unable to use his arm or leg. He could talk, but it was difficult to understand everything he said.

I gave her that information and said, "It looks like he has pneumonia. I'll get some blood work and an X-ray, and then he'll probably need to be admitted. Why?"

"Was there somebody else in the room? Did he have a friend with him?" she asked.

"Yes, there was another man there, and I guess he was his friend," I answered. "He helped me communicate with him when Mr. Barkley would have trouble finding the right word or didn't seem to understand what I was saying."

"That would be Frank Witherspoon," she said, nodding her head as if that was something I was supposed to know.

I waited for her to say something else, but she just looked at me for a moment and then walked over to one of the stools near the counter. She sat down and took a deep breath.

"Have a seat," she told me, rolling the other stool over in my direction. This was really strange. I had never seen Virginia like this before, and I didn't know what to expect next.

Following her instruction, I grabbed the stool and sat down.

"Dr. Lesslie," she began. Her voice was somehow different, and it surprised me. She was speaking quietly, but with a definite seriousness, and there was something else there. It was a gentleness, something I couldn't remember hearing before. "Do you believe in angels?"

I sat there, looking at this ex-military nurse, with her starched and stiff white uniform and the pointed white cap on her head. This was a woman who intimidated most of the physicians on the medical staff and who never backed down from the biggest, most belligerent troublemaker in the ER. In fact, with her feet apart and her hands on her hips, she never failed to back down *all* of them.

And here she was, sitting in front of me and asking me this question. I studied her face for a moment and knew that her question was serious. And I knew she really wanted to know what I thought.

"I do, and I think if you work in the ER long enough, you *have* to."

"You know I'm not talking about wings and harps and halos and all of that," she replied, smiling a little. "Although I'm not ruling it out entirely."

She chuckled a little, and I found myself relaxing, intrigued by this conversation. We had never talked like this before.

"Do you remember the little Carpenter girl?" she asked me. "Emmy, I think her name was. The child with the leukemia?"

It had only been a few months, and I clearly remembered the six-year-old.

"Yes, I was here the last time she came in," I answered. "You were here too, if I remember correctly. It was just two days before she died."

"And do you remember what she told us that morning?"

I tried to focus, struggling to remember anything Emmy might have said, something that would have stuck in my mind. But I had been busy, in and out of the room, trying to get things lined up for her admission and talking with her specialists.

"I don't know," I answered finally. "I don't remember anything unusual."

"Well, I was in the room with her, and she was lying on the stretcher, as calm and peaceful as always. And then she asked me if I saw them."

Virginia paused and put her hand to her chin. Then she took another deep breath, sighed, and went on. "I asked her. 'Who?' and she pointed to the end of the stretcher and said, 'Those beautiful ladies.'"

Virginia's voice was trembling, and tears were forming in her eyes. But she continued.

"I told her I couldn't see them, but I knew they were there. And Emmy said, 'They like you, Miss G.' And Dr. Lesslie, I can't explain it, but I had this feeling, it was the most peaceful…"

She couldn't go on, and I waited.

Finally, she looked up at me. "And then that little girl smiled and said, 'Miss G, they told me not to worry and that everything will be alright. They said Jesus knows my name. And he knows yours too.'"

Once more she was silent, and I just looked at her. And then I wiped away the tears from my own eyes.

Virginia sat up straighter, slapped her knees, and leaned closer to me.

"Now, let me tell you about Jim Barkley and Frank Witherspoon, the two men in room 4."

"Ms. Granger, if it's anything like what you just told me about Emmy, I'm going to need a box of Kleenex."

"Well, there's some behind you on the counter," she said, smiling. "But this is important, and I want to share it with you."

I settled on my stool, and Virginia told me about these two special men.

Jim Barkley and Frank Witherspoon were both in their late seventies, and both were veterans of the Second World War. They had the common bond of having served in the U.S. Third Army under General George S. Patton, fighting in different units in northern Africa, Sicily, and finally in France. They didn't actually meet until years later, when they each moved to Rock Hill with their wives. Jim taught English at Winthrop University, while Frank was a financial consultant with one of the large banks in Charlotte. They attended the same Presbyterian church, and that's where they were first introduced to each other.

It was their wives who first got them together. They were in the same women's organization and quickly realized they had a lot in common. Jim and Frank realized they had a lot in common as well and soon became fast friends. The two couples spent a lot of time together, and when Jim's wife became ill, Frank and Betty were there for her, and for him.

When she died, the three of them became inseparable. And then Betty, Frank's wife, got sick. None of the doctors could tell them where the cancer had started, but by the time it was diagnosed, it was too late. And the end came quickly.

"Betty Witherspoon was a good friend of mine," Virginia told me. "And she was a good woman. Right before she died, she talked with Jim and asked him to look after her husband. She knew he would be lost for a while and would need his friend. And Jim promised he would do just that. Funny how things work out, though. It turned out that Frank would be the one looking after Jim."

"You mean, after he had his stroke?" I asked her.

"Well, it started before that. Jim has had a lot of medical problems the past couple of years, and the stroke was just the latest."

She told me how Frank had always been at Jim's side, no matter what happened, no matter how difficult.

"After his stroke, Jim couldn't do anything for himself," she told me. "But Frank was always there. Jim didn't have anybody else, and Frank knew it, and he was the only one looking after him. But he wouldn't have it any other way. At one point, some of us talked with him about finding a retirement home for Jim, but Frank wouldn't hear of it. There are some good facilities here in Rock Hill, but he was determined to keep his friend at home and take care of him. A year or two ago that changed, and Jim moved into Westminster Towers. And you know what? Frank moved in right beside him. And he still takes care of him. You're not going to see one without the other."

She stopped and looked over at me, and I thought her story was finished. I was wrong.

"Dr. Lesslie, there are different kinds of angels in this world, and I believe the Lord puts them in our lives when we need them most, at just the right time and at just the right place. For Emmy, it was those two ladies standing at the foot of her stretcher. That's what she needed right then. And for Jim…well, Frank is *his* angel. Don't you see? He's more than just a friend. I don't know how Jim would have survived after his wife died. And you know, I'm not sure how Frank would have survived without Jim. It's all more than I can understand, but I know it's all real. And I *do* believe in angels, Dr. Lesslie. You just have to keep your eyes open. They're out there and they're with us. I know that for certain."

She looked at me, not saying anything. I wasn't sure what to say to her—my mind was struggling with some of my own experiences, and with hearing this story of the men in room 4.

Virginia stood up slowly, stretched, and headed for the door.

"Come on, Dr. Lesslie. We have work to do."

"Ms. Granger," I said hesitantly. "Wait a minute."

She stopped in the doorway and turned to face me.

"What is it?" she asked.

"I want to ask you something. No, I want to tell you something, and then ask you what you think about it."

"Sure, go ahead," she replied, walking back into the room.

I was still sitting on the stool, and I put my hands on my knees, leaned forward, and looked down at the tiled floor.

Then, looking up at her, I said, "Several months ago we had a yard sale at the house. You know we're moving, and we were trying to get rid of twenty-five years of stuff that was just taking up space. Anyway, we had things spread out all over the house and out in the driveway. And we had people everywhere. They were milling around the kitchen and dining room, and at one point you could barely move. Well, I was trying to stand out of the way, over in a corner, when this man walked up to me. I didn't know him, had never seen him in my life. But he just walked up as if he knew me and started talking. He was sort of scruffy and hadn't shaved in a while."

"This your place?" he asked me.

"Yes, it is," I told him. "Are you looking for anything in particular?"

He just stood there and sort of cocked his head, staring at me. He acted like he knew me, but again, I had never seen him before.

Then he said, "Tell me, what is your ministry?"

I wasn't sure I had heard him correctly, and I said, "My ministry?"

"Yes. What is your ministry?" he repeated.

I stood there and thought about that for a minute. What *was* my ministry? Maybe I should tell him I was a doctor and *that* was my ministry. But somehow I knew that wasn't what he was asking me. He wanted to know how I was serving and living out my faith. He wasn't trying to put me on the spot. It was almost like he was letting me put myself on the spot.

"Well," I continued, "you can figure I got uncomfortable and was struggling for an answer.

"And what did you tell him?" Virginia asked.

"Barbara was calling for me and wanted a price on something in the living room. I told the man I would be right back, and I went over to help her, and when I got back, he was gone. I looked all over the house and out in the yard, but I couldn't find him anywhere."

"Hmm," she murmured. "And what did you make of that?"

"Nothing at first," I answered. "I was busy with the yard sale, and there was stuff going on. There's *always* stuff going on, isn't there? But the more I thought about that guy, the more I began to wonder about his question. What *is* my ministry? That's become an important issue for me, and one that I'm struggling with."

I was silent, and looked up at her for a response.

"And what question do you have of me?" she asked gently. "Do you want to know if I think that man was an angel? Was he placed in your life at exactly that moment to cause you to have these questions? Could that be the way the Lord sometimes works in our lives?"

I thought about what she was saying and just sat there.

"We both know the answer, don't we?" she said, stepping closer and putting a hand on my shoulder. "You just have to keep your eyes and ears open. And your heart."

She turned and headed out of trauma, stopping at the door and flipping off the light switch.

"Come on," she said to me, adjusting her cap and smoothing the front of her dress. "You need to take care of Jim Barkley in room 4."

To one who has faith,
no explanation is necessary.

—THOMAS AQUINAS (1225–1274)

Revelation

The next morning, Virginia met with Bill Chalmers. I wasn't coming in until that night, so she called me at home and told me about their conversation.

"Bill's initial response was exactly the same as yours and mine," she told me. "He kept wondering what we could do for Amy. He really feels bad about that."

"He should," I responded. "But I guess we all should. What did you tell him?"

"Nothing, really. I just let him talk, and eventually he came to the right conclusion. He's going to call her and apologize and ask her to come back to the hospital. I just hope she'll listen to him."

I did too, but Amy had been deeply hurt by all that had happened. It would be a lot for her to put aside, and a lot for her to forgive. I wasn't sure I would be able to do it.

"And what did he say about the drug problem? We're not going to see Walter Stevens nosing around the ER again, are we?" I asked her.

"No, we don't have to worry about that," Virginia chuckled. "Bill knows he made a mistake there. He's not any too happy about the information Walter gave him last time. He told me he was going to handle this personally. And I got the distinct sense that he's going to be very cautious and make sure it's handled correctly. He asked if I thought we should get DHEC involved."

She waited, giving me a chance to express my thoughts.

"DHEC does need to know about this," I told her. "I was surprised before when Stevens didn't contact them. They should be able to give us some good advice and help Bill avoid any more mistakes."

"That's exactly what I told him," Virginia said. "Looks like I did a good job raisin' you up after all."

"Huh," I grunted, my mind having returned to Amy Connors and how we could best help her. "Do you think we ought to give Amy a call in a couple of days, after Bill has a chance to contact her?"

"No, I don't think that's a good idea," she said thoughtfully. "Let's see what comes of his talk with her. Maybe it will work itself out, but maybe not. What I want you to be thinking about is how we should approach Darren Adler, or if we should just wait and let things play out."

I had already been thinking about that. With Bill Chalmers in charge now, it gave us an excuse to step back and let things unfold. But it wasn't my nature to run from a problem, or to be patient. However, I knew patience was what was needed here.

"Let me think about that and we'll talk the next time I see you."

"Fine," she told me. "And have a good night. The ER was busy when I left."

She hung up and I got ready to head to the hospital.

6:55 p.m. As the ambulance entrance doors swung open, I immediately sensed that something unusual was going on. Susan Everett looked up at me wide-eyed from behind the nurses' station. Then Lori Davidson burst out from behind the curtain of room 4, heading toward the medicine room. When she saw me, she quickly turned and hurried over to where I stood.

"You need to go help Dr. Kennick in 4," she said a little breathlessly. Then she shook her head and said, "I don't know what's going on. But please, see if you can help."

She glanced over her shoulder at Susan and called out to the secretary, "We need lab over in 4—stat!" Then without saying anything else, she disappeared into the medicine room.

I had never seen Lori like this. She was upset about something, and was distracted. I looked over at the closed curtain of room 4 and decided to talk with her before going over there.

She was standing in front of the narcotics cabinet reaching for some vials of medication when I stepped up beside her.

"What's the matter?" I asked her. "What's going on?"

She had some syringes and needles in her hand and put these down on the counter. Then she turned to me and said, "There's a man in 4 with back pain—a kidney stone, it looks like. And Dr. Kennick has been trying to get rid of his pain for over an hour. Nothing is helping. He's had almost 30 mgs of morphine and no relief. Now I'm getting him some more. But something's just not right."

That was a lot of morphine. But sometimes kidney stones took a lot of pain medicine.

"What's not right?" I asked her.

She was flushed, and a confused look passed over her face.

"It's almost like we're giving him saline IV and not morphine," she answered. "It doesn't seem to faze his pain. And he's a reasonable guy, not a drug-seeker or one of our regulars."

She looked back up into the narcotics cabinet. "I just don't understand it," she sighed.

"Is someone in there with Dr. Kennick?" I asked her.

"Yeah, Darren Adler. But he's been tied up with the patient, starting an IV and stuff. He hasn't had a chance to leave the room. Dr. Kennick had to come in here and get most of the morphine herself. I was getting some medicine for a patient in OBS and I showed her where it was. But now she's getting upset and frustrated. That's why you need to go help her," she insisted. "I don't think she knows what to do."

"Okay," I said, turning and walking behind the nurses' station toward room 4. I was almost there, when the curtain suddenly opened and Darren stuck his head out.

"Susan!" he called. Then he saw me standing in front of him he said, "Great! Dr. Lesslie, come on in here, we need some help!"

"Susan!" he turned again to the secretary. "We need a portable X-ray in here stat!"

I stepped around Darren and over to the stretcher. Liz Kennick was standing by the counter, making some notes on the patient's chart. Looking up at me as I entered the room, she said, "Good, glad you're here, Robert." Then she looked back down at the clipboard.

"Dan Perkins," she said to me, her voice steady and businesslike. "Fifty-seven-year-old with left flank pain and blood in his urine. No history of kidney stones, but that's what it looks like. I'm just trying to get his pain relieved." She didn't look up, but kept writing on his chart.

I turned to the man on the stretcher and stepped closer to him.

He looked up at me, his face pale and covered with sweat. There was obvious pain in his eyes, but also fear.

His hands were desperately clutching the raised rails of the stretcher, and his arms were shaking a little.

"Doc, I need some help," he said quietly, his voice trembling. "This pain is killing me."

I put my hand on his left arm. His skin was cool and clammy, and I asked Darren, "What's his blood pressure?"

"100 over 60, last time we checked," he told me. "That was about twenty minutes ago. Want me to get another one?"

"Not right now," Liz answered without turning around.

Darren looked at me questioningly. Without saying anything, I nodded once, and he leaned over to get the blood-pressure cuff out of its holder on the wall.

"When did this pain start?" I asked Mr. Perkins.

"About half an hour before I got here," he answered, glancing up at the clock on the wall beside him. "That'd make it about two hours ago."

Two hours? What has Liz been doing all this time?

"Have you had any relief from the pain?" I asked him.

"No, not at all," he said quietly. "It's still killing me."

Darren moved beside him and said, "Let's try to sit you up a little, Mr. Perkins. I'm going to check your blood pressure again."

When the nurse raised the head of the bed and Perkins tried to move, he let out a loud scream.

"Aaghh! I can't!"

He clutched the rails of the bed even tighter and looked up at me, pleading.

"Don't make me move!" he begged. "I can't stand it!"

Liz spun around, saw Adler trying to take the man's blood pressure, and demanded, "Darren, just what are you doing! I told you we didn't need to do that now!"

Then she looked at me with daggers flying and said, "Do you want to take over here?"

Her eyes moved to the clock on the wall. "It's time for me to go, anyway. So here, he's all yours."

She was trying to hand me the man's clipboard, but I just stood and stared at her. I had never seen her behave like this before.

Then it hit me.

I whirled around and looked down again at Mr. Perkins. He wasn't moving at all. Instead, he was desperately trying to remain absolutely still.

That's what wasn't making any sense! A person with a kidney stone *can't* keep still. Their pain won't let them. They will pace and squirm and move around, anything in an attempt to find some relief. This man wasn't doing any of that. Instead, he was doing just the opposite. He was trying *not* to move.

"80 over 60," Darren told us, putting the blood-pressure cuff back up.

"Probably just the morphine we've been giving him," Liz muttered from behind me. "Here, take this. I'm outta here." She pushed the clipboard into the small of my back.

"Just a minute, Liz," I said without turning around.

Then I moved right beside the stretcher and reached out, gently placing my hand on Mr. Perkins's abdomen.

"Are you having any pain here?" I asked him, pressing down a little, palpating different areas of his belly. He was slender and easy to examine.

"No, the pain is in my back," he told me, his eyes searching mine. "Aaghh! That hurt!" he hollered, reaching down to move my hand away.

"Liz," I said. "Come over here and feel this."

"I'm off duty," she replied curtly, turning to leave the room.

"Liz, come over here and feel this." This time my voice was low and firm, and there was no mistaking my intent.

She hesitated, but only briefly. Then she moved over beside me.

"Where?" she scoffed. It was obvious she was becoming increasingly annoyed. Darren looked up at her and then over to me.

"Put your hand right here," I directed her, pointing to an area just above and to the right of his navel.

"I don't feel—" She stopped mid-sentence and her entire body tensed. Then she placed both hands on the man's abdomen and began to examine him more carefully.

She was feeling his aorta. It was enlarged, forcefully pulsating, and was about to burst, if it hadn't already.

It all came together. This man had an abdominal aortic aneurysm and it was getting ready to blow. *This* was causing his back pain, and not a kidney stone. And it explained his low blood pressure, the blood in his urine, and his determination to remain completely still. He needed to be in the OR, probably an hour ago.

"Did you feel his belly when he first came in?" I asked her quietly.

Across the stretcher, I saw Darren look up at Liz, waiting for her response. He had been in the room from the first moment Dan Perkins had come to the ER.

"Of course I did," she answered defensively. Darren shook his head and looked down at the patient.

I studied her for a moment and then turned to Darren.

"We need to get in touch with the vascular surgeon on call. And we'll need another IV, some blood typed and crossed, and a portable chest X-ray. I'll send Lori in to help."

Then stepping toward the entrance, I turned to Liz and said, "Come out here with me for just a second."

She followed me as we moved out of the room and to the back of the nurses' station.

Facing her and carefully considering my words, I said, "Liz, we all make mistakes. The key is to be sure we learn something from them. And—"

"Look!" she exclaimed angrily, then pointed her finger at me, not more than an inch from my nose. "If you're going to hand me that stuff again about *making assumptions*, you can just save your breath."

Over her shoulder, I could see Susan and Lori turn and stare at the two of us, their mouths hanging open.

"Just calm down, Liz," I said quietly, reaching up and slowly moving her hand from in front of my face.

"I'm not the one who needs to calm down!" she yelled. "So I missed an aneurysm! What's the big deal? You've never missed anything before?"

She was quickly spinning out of control, her body shaking and her face a deep red.

"Liz—"

"Don't *Liz* me!" Her hand went up again, this time with her palm in my face. "I'm outta here!"

She turned, walked around the nurses' station, and disappeared down the hallway.

I was hot, and was about to follow her back to our office when I remembered Dan Perkins. Quickly stepping over to Susan and Lori, I told them what we needed. Within a few minutes, the surgeon was on his way to the ER and Mr. Perkins was almost ready for the operating room.

"There, that should do it," I told Lori, sliding the man's chart over to her. "I'll be right back."

She looked up at me but didn't say anything as I headed down the hallway.

I was still angry, still trying to get control of my emotions. Liz had really ticked me off, and I was wondering what in the world had flipped her switch.

She was standing by one of our bookshelves when I walked into the office. Her head jerked in my direction, and she began fumbling with some of the heavy texts on one of the upper shelves.

"What do you want?" she sputtered angrily, looking first at me and then back up at the bookshelf. She clumsily tried to straighten up the jumbled books but quickly gave up and turned to face me.

"Look, if you're going to try to lecture me, I don't want to hear it!"

Where has all of this anger come from?

"Liz, why don't you just hold on and have a seat for a few minutes," I told her as calmly as I could. "We need to talk."

"There's nothing to talk about!" she almost yelled. "I told you, I'm off duty and I'm getting out of here!"

Then she backed away and reached down for her sweater, quickly putting it on. She must have just taken off her lab coat and tossed it onto one of the chairs in front of the desk.

But I had seen it. And I stood there, looking into her eyes.

She had seen my glance and now turned her head away from me, patting the sleeves of her sweater. She became more agitated and started looking around the office for something. When she finally spotted her shoulder bag, she walked over, grabbed it, and headed for the door.

"Liz," I said quietly.

Her hand was on the doorknob and she hesitated for just an instant.

"I saw your arm."

She stood there, staring down at the handle, and her shoulders slumped. Then she sighed heavily and dropped her bag to the floor.

She didn't say anything. She didn't have to. The needle tracks in her left elbow said it all.

How have we missed this? Surely something *should have tipped us off.*

Then I remembered some of the simple mistakes she had been making, and her lack of patience with some of our "regulars." But this had escalated so quickly. It had not even been a couple of months since we had first noticed the missing Vistaril.

It's been Liz all along. But what about Amy? How could Liz have…

The shock of all this was beginning to subside and now I was more than angry—I was livid. We had brought this young woman into our midst, into our family, and she had almost destroyed it. Maybe she *had* destroyed it.

I wanted to walk over, grab her by her shoulders, and shake her until…

When I looked at her again, she was still standing by the door with her head hanging on her chest. She had put her arms around herself and was slowly rocking from side to side.

I turned back to the shelves and looked up at the toppled medical books. Reaching up, I moved them aside and felt behind them. When I turned around, Liz was looking at me, her eyes reddened and her lips trembling.

I opened my hand and showed her four syringes. They were each filled with a clear liquid, the morphine intended for Dan Perkins.

Liz Kennick collapsed into one of the chairs, her head in her hands, and she began to sob uncontrollably.

I walked around behind the desk, picked up the phone, dialed the nurses' station, and said, "Susan, would you ask Lori to come back to our office."

21

Redemption

A few days later, Virginia and I were in the medicine room, discussing the tumultuous events of the past few weeks.

It had taken us several phone calls, but with the help of the state medical board we were able to locate a drug rehab center for Liz Kennick. She was on her way to a facility in Virginia that specialized in the treatment of professionals, and she had a tough road ahead and some hard work to do.

She knew that, and she knew her medical license would be revoked. Whatever flaw in her character, whatever weakness that had allowed her to fall into this trap, it would have to be overcome if she was to continue a career in medicine. More important than that, it would need to be overcome if she was to regain control of her life.

"I hope that young woman knows how lucky she is," Virginia said, shuffling through some purchase orders. "The hospital had every right to press charges against her, and she might be looking at jail time in addition to losing her license. She has Bill Chalmers to thank for that."

"Still, she's going to be paying a heavy price for what she's done," I told her.

"Hmm," Virginia grumbled. "She's leaving some real damage behind her. And speaking of Bill Chalmers, he came by my office yesterday."

I was leaning against the counter, watching her do her paperwork.

"What was that about?" I asked her.

"It was interesting," she said, putting her papers aside and looking up at me. "He wanted to talk about Amy Connors. He had tried to call her a couple of times, after all of this happened, but never talked with her. He had left messages but she never returned his calls. So then he found out where she lives and went to see her."

"He *what?*" I exclaimed. "When was the last time—"

"I know," she interrupted. "When have you ever heard of that happening? And it may never happen again. But he was determined to talk with her, and that's what he did. He drove out to her house."

"Wow. I never would have expected that. I hope Amy's husband wasn't at home. That would have been some fireworks!"

"You're right about that," she laughed. "But Charlie wasn't there. It was just Amy, and they talked for a good while. He apologized as best he could and asked her to come back to the hospital."

"I hope she knows how much it took for him to do that," I said. "It was the right thing...but still, that surprises me. How did she respond?"

"He told me he couldn't be sure," she explained. "She listened to him, and she accepted his apology. But she told him she'd have to think about ever coming back to the hospital and the ER. He didn't sound too hopeful. Oh, and he told her about Walter Stevens."

"What about Stevens?" I asked. I hadn't heard anything about the vice president and didn't know what she was talking about.

"You need to pay more attention to the hospital grapevine," she said knowingly. "Stevens has been given a sideways promotion—actually it's a *demotion*, and everyone knows it. Bill relieved him of his duties and put him in charge of facilities management."

"You mean housekeeping and making sure the grass is mowed?" I chuckled.

"It's a little more than that, but yes," she replied. "Bill's idea is to give him some time to mature a little, to gain more management experience."

"You mean, in a place where he's not going to mess up so badly?" I asked.

"That's the general idea," Virginia said, picking up her paperwork once more. "And I think it's a good one."

There was a tapping on the door and both of us looked over.

It was Darren Adler, and he was standing there in his street clothes.

"Ms. Granger, Dr. Lesslie. Good morning," he said politely.

"Good morning, Darren," Virginia said. I detected a sadness in her voice, or maybe it was resignation.

"You haven't changed your mind, have you?" I asked him.

"No, I haven't done that," he answered.

I studied him for a moment, hoping for a different response. But none was offered.

Reaching into one of my lab-coat pockets, I took out a sealed envelope and handed it to him.

"Here you go," I said quietly. "And if you need anything else, just let me know."

It was a letter of recommendation. Darren was applying for a job in one of the ERs in Charlotte and had asked me for this a few days ago.

He was leaving Rock Hill General, determined to move on from all that had happened. In spite of everything Virginia and I could say, and in spite of our apologies, he didn't think he could get past the thought of our having lost faith in him. But I knew it was more than that. He had lost faith in us.

"Maybe someday," he had said when Virginia told him he would always have a place in our ER.

Here was another casualty of Liz Kennick's terrible wrongdoing.

"Thanks, Dr. Lesslie," he said, taking the envelope from my hand. "I'm sure I'll be seeing you guys around."

Without another word, he turned and walked out of the department and out of the hospital.

Virginia sighed and looked at me, slowly shaking her head. Then I saw her look down at her watch and step over to the window overlooking the parking lot. She was scanning the area, looking for something.

"Well, would you look at that?" she said quietly in exaggerated surprise.

I stepped over behind her and looked out the window.

"What are you talking about?" I asked her, not noticing anything unusual.

"Over there," she answered, pointing to the employee parking area.

It was a big silver truck, and it had just come to a stop in one of the parking spaces.

"I know what you're thinking," I told her, turning back around, determined not to be disappointed once again. "And it's not who you think it is."

"Oh yeah?"

There was something in her voice that made me turn around one more time and move closer to the window. The truck door was opening, and out stepped...Amy Connors!

"What!" I exclaimed. "Did you know about this?"

Virginia winked at me and said, "Aren't you supposed to be somewhere?"

I looked at the window and then back at Virginia. Then I muttered something that didn't make any sense and headed for the door.

Amy had just walked through the ambulance entrance and was headed straight for the nurses' station. I hurried over, intercepting her before she got there.

"Amy!" I said. Then I hugged her. I had always respected and loved this woman, but never more than in this one moment. It had taken a lot of courage and faith for her to walk through those doors. And a lot of forgiveness.

We just stood there, with every eye in the department focused on the two of us.

Then smiling up at me she said, "Get on with yourself."

She stepped back from me, and suddenly the department erupted in applause. Standing in the triage doorway was Jeff Ryan, hootin' and hollerin'. Clara Adams was clapping loudly while tears rolled down her cheeks. And Virginia Granger stood in the doorway of the medicine room, feet apart, arms crossed, and nodding her head.

Amy looked over at the nurses' station and at Lori Davidson, sitting behind it.

"And Lori, you need to get out of my chair. We've got work to do!"

22

Phoenix Rising

11:15 a.m.—6 months later. "Amy, we're going to need an ultra-sound on the woman in 5. 'Right upper quadrant pain—gallbladder disease.'"

"Got it," she replied, reaching up for the chart. "Anything else?"

I slid the clipboard across the counter and said, "Nope. That should do it."

The door to triage opened and Lori Davidson and I turned around.

Patsy Wilson was pushing a wheelchair into the department and stopped right in front of us.

"This is Sarah Alpert," she told us. "It seems that she slipped on her carpet this morning and might have broken her wrist."

I glanced down and noticed the temporary splint on her left wrist. It was already swollen and bruised, and it looked like Patsy was going to be right.

The elderly woman in the chair looked up at me and said, "Dr. Lesslie, is that you?"

Looking closer, I now recognized her. She had been one of the matriarchs of our church when we first moved to Rock Hill, a great lady and a great teacher. She had broken a hip several years ago and was having a hard time getting around. I hadn't seen her in a while.

"Yes, it's me, Mrs. Alpert," I answered, reaching down and taking her uninjured hand in mine.

"Well, I'm mighty glad you're here this morning to take care of me," she said, smiling.

"You know this guy and you're still glad to see him?" Patsy said in mock surprise.

"Why of *course* I am," Sarah said, squeezing my hand. "He's always been such a fine young man."

"Are you sure we're talking about the same person?" Patsy persisted, making faces at me from behind Mrs. Alpert.

"Honey, don't make me get out of this chair. I've still got one good arm," she said laughing, still quick-witted and still lighthearted.

"It's okay, Mrs. Alpert," I told her. "I'll take care of Patsy. Let's get you back to ortho and get an X-ray of that wrist."

"Thank you, Dr. Lesslie," she replied, settling back in the wheelchair and pointing down the hallway.

"Okay, Mrs. Alpert," Patsy said to her patient. "Let's rock and roll."

When they were out of hearing, Lori said, "It's great having Patsy back. Almost like old times."

"You're right about that," I agreed, chuckling quietly.

The phone rang, and Amy picked it up.

"Rock Hill General ER. This is Amy Connors."

Lori and I were writing on a couple of charts and weren't paying any attention to Amy and her phone call. Not until she said, "Hello, Dr. Kennick."

We each stopped what we were doing and stared across the counter at her.

She sank back into her chair and twirled a pencil between her right index finger and thumb.

"That will be fine," she said into the receiver.

She sat there, listening and occasionally nodding her head. "Charlie gets off about 5 or 5:30, so 6 ought to be about right."

More silence, and then, "Okay, we'll see you then. Yeah, here he is." She sat forward in her chair and held the receiver out to me.

"It's for you," she told me. "Dr. Kennick."

I looked at the receiver, then over to Lori. She seemed as confused as I was, but when I just stood there, she poked me in the side with her elbow and motioned for me to take the phone.

"Here," Amy whispered, thrusting the receiver at me.

I took it from her, covered the mouthpiece, and made a silent gesture with my head for them to give me some privacy. They just smiled, obviously not going anywhere.

I gave up and put the phone to my ear.

"Liz, this is Robert," I said, not knowing what to say next.

She immediately jumped in and said, "Robert, I know you're busy, but I just need to say a couple of things."

I hadn't talked with her since she'd left the ER and was admitted into rehab. We had heard a few things here and there, and that she seemed to be doing okay, but nothing concrete. This phone call was coming out of the clear blue.

"Sure, Liz," I told her. "It's not too busy right now. What's on your mind?"

"I just want you to know what's going on with me," she began, her voice calm and sure. "But first, I want to apologize, and tell you how sorry I am for what happened in the ER, with the drugs. I let you down, and I let myself down. And I still can't believe I would ever put a patient at risk. Most of all though, I let Amy Connors down. I let her take the fall for me, and I knew what I was doing. With everything I've had to deal with, that has been the hardest part."

Her voice was trembling and she was silent for a moment. I glanced at Lori and then at Amy. They couldn't hear any of this and just looked at me.

"Rehab was tough," she continued, her voice once again controlled. "But those people really knew what they were doing. I know I'm an addict, and that I'll struggle with that knowledge every day for the rest of my life. But I'll never forget what I did."

"It all seemed to happen so fast," I said, still wondering how we had missed this.

"You're right, and that's what the counselors said. I think it was the pressure of medical school and my residency, and the pressure I put on myself because of my parents. Then with my new position at Rock Hill General, I wanted everything to be just right. I did a good job with *that* one, didn't I?"

"Tell me what you're doing now," I asked her. "Are you working somewhere?"

"I am," she answered, her voice brightening as we changed the subject. "I've been out of rehab for a little more than five weeks, and I started in an urgent-care center just outside of Richmond. It's low-volume and low-stress, and I think it's just what I need right now. I want to get back into the ER, but it needs to be at the right time."

There was silence, and I looked down at Amy.

"Liz, seems like you've been talking with Amy Connors," I ventured.

Amy's eyebrows rose, and she looked up at me with reddening eyes.

"We've talked a couple of times," she told me. "She was the first person I contacted, but it took a while before I could...before I could get up the courage. She's such an amazing woman. I should never have been afraid to call her. But yes, we've been talking. I wanted her to know how sorry I am for the pain I caused her, and that I caused her family. I can only hope and pray that someday she'll be able to find a way to forgive me."

"I think she will, Liz," I told her quietly.

I looked down again at Amy and our eyes met. This time, there were tears in mine.

"And you're right," I added. "She *is* an amazing woman."

"And what about you, Robert? Do you think you can ever...?"

Her voice trailed off and I realized how difficult all of this was for her.

"Don't worry about me, Liz. We just want you to get well and to be strong and to—"

"But can you *forgive* me?" she asked again.

This was hard, and I wasn't sure what to say.

Who was I to forgive this woman? I knew that she needed to find forgiveness, and that she would have to find a way to forgive herself. But she was asking *me*.

The hurt and anger and disappointment I had felt were trying to resurface, but they were powerless before Amy Connors and now before a contrite and sincere Liz Kennick. Who was I *not* to forgive this woman?

"Of course I forgive you, Liz."

I thought I heard sobbing on the other end of the phone. After a few moments, Liz cleared her throat and said, "I'd really like to come by and see you guys sometime, if that's okay. First though, I'm going to sit down with Amy and Charlie, and just talk. We need to do that. But later…"

"Whenever you're ready, Liz. We'll be here."

I handed the phone back to Amy and she hung it up.

I took a deep breath and slowly let it out. What had just happened was important—for all of us.

The three of us stood there and didn't say anything. We didn't *need* to say anything.

From across the department, we heard Virginia Granger's office door open and we all looked over.

She stepped out, planted her feet wide apart, and put her hands on her hips.

Then once again she stared straight at me over those black-rimmed bifocals, and with pursed lips said, "Dr. Lesslie, we need to have a *word*!"

Oh, no. What had I done now?

"He will wipe away every tear from their eyes.
There will be no more death or mourning
or crying or pain,
for the old order of things has passed away."
He who was seated on the throne said,
"I am making everything new!"

REVELATION 21:4-5

Notes

Page 42: "…we will be present with the Lord." See 2 Corinthians 5:6-8.

Page 72: "Let my heart be broken…" Quote by Robert Pierce (1914–1978).

About the Author

D r. Robert Lesslie, bestselling author of *Angels in the ER, Angels on Call,* and *Angels and Heroes,* is a physician who lives and actively practices medicine in Rock Hill, South Carolina. Board-certified in both emergency medicine and occupational medicine, he is the co-owner of two busy urgent care/occupational clinics.

For more than 25 years, Dr. Lesslie worked in and directed several of the busiest ERs in the Charlotte, North Carolina, area. He also served as medical director of the emergency department at Rock Hill General Hospital for almost 15 years. During his tenure as medical director, he received the American Medical Association's Continuing Education Award. He also traveled around the country, giving lively, innovative lectures to the Emergency Nurses Association at their annual meetings in major cities.

For seven years, Dr. Lesslie wrote a weekly medical column for *The Charlotte Observer* presenting a wide variety of topics, both medical and editorial. He also pens a regular column on medical, philosophical, and personal topics for the *YC,* a monthly publication in York County, North Carolina.

Dr. Lesslie enjoys the fast-paced environment of the ER and the need to make rapid and accurate diagnoses. He views his medical career as an opportunity to go beyond simply diagnosing and treating individual patients. For him, it is a way to fulfill a higher calling by meeting the real physical and emotional needs of his patients.

An active member of his home church in Rock Hill, Dr.

Lesslie serves as an elder, and he and his wife, Barbara, teach Sunday school and sing in the church choir. They are also involved with an outreach program for disabled/handicapped individuals, Camp Joy, where Dr. Lesslie serves as the camp physician for a week each summer. He also enjoys mentoring high-school and college students considering a career in medicine.

Dr. Lesslie and his wife, Barbara, have been married for more than 35 years. Together they have raised four children—Lori, Amy, Robbie, and Jeffrey—and are now enjoying five grandchildren. In his spare time, Dr. Lesslie enjoys gardening, golf, hunting, reading, and bagpiping.